Friedhelm Lessmeier

The British Shorthair Cat

Everything About Acquisition, Care, Nutrition, Behavior, Health Care, Breeding, and Showing

Color photos by
Ulrike Schanz

Illustrations by
Renate Holzner

Consulting Editor:
Karen Leigh Davis

BARRON'S

Contents

Chasing a ball is a favorite pastime for kittens and cats alike.

Preface

The British shorthair is lovingly called a "teddy bear" by its fanciers. Regardless of what this attribute might suggest, this feline is not merely a cat to cuddle. Breed hallmarks include an uncomplicated, even-tempered, friendly, and affectionate character in a cat that adapts easily, learns readily, possesses a robust body, and low-maintenance habits. Small wonder that this is one of the most popular breeds of all purebreds!

Friedhelm Lessmeier, internationally known for his successful breed of Bavarians Blues, addresses in this book important questions on the proper care and handling of this delightful breed. You can expect to learn from him how to find a serious and reputable breeder and what to look for when you go shopping for a healthy, "picture perfect" British shorthair kitten.

In addition, the author incorporates tips on how to help a new cat adapt to its new home, as well as how to provide good care and nutrition. If you are interested in breeding or showing cats, you will find those sections of the book useful as well. The book also contains several illustrated HOW-TO sections that deal with training, activities, care, and first aid.

Photos specifically created for this book enhance and complete a lively image of the British shorthair "teddy bear." The author and the publisher wish you much enjoyment with your British shorthair cat.

*Please pay
special attention
to the important
advice on (p. 63).*

Understanding British Shorthair Cats

British shorthair kittens' eyes are blue until they reach about six weeks old; then, slowly, the typical copper color begins to develop.

From Wild Cat to Domestic Cat to Purebred Cat

The history of purebred cats is relatively short, considering that cats were domesticated only 5,000 years ago. Felines are among our most recent house pets. Other animals, such as dogs and horses, had long been our steadfast companions, while the arrival of house cats did not take place until we settled down, exchanged tents for houses, and built storage barns. The establishment of these food storage buildings attracted less welcome rats and mice, but fortunately, felines followed soon afterward. In fact, cats did not arrive on the scene just to be close to humans, they came to be close to the dinner table. The unwelcome rodents that plagued the grain stores turned out to be easy prey for the cats, so, for quite practical reasons, cats became increasingly welcome to humans, and domestication slowly took place.

Today's cat fanciers might rephrase this historic scenario by saying, "Cats decided to tolerate humans and allowed us to live with them." Our four-legged friends, however, did not always enjoy an easy life with us. At times in our history, cats have been revered as godlike creatures, while at other times, they have been cursed as devils and witches and even killed for their innocent association with occult elements.

Ancestry of the British Shorthair

The historical lineage of the British shorthair cat abounds with legends. We cannot be truly certain whether this cat originated centuries ago from cats that were bred by French monks who attempted to find a way to control a rat plague, or whether these cats arrived as "stowaway passengers" on ships from the Far East. Certain only is the fact that a hardy breed of shorthaired cats was bred in France under the name of "Chartreux." At about the same time in England, an almost identical breed was being developed called the "British shorthair."

Chartreux: The British shorthair appeared in France during the eighteenth century under the name, *Chat des Chartreux*. During the early half of that century, the Léger sisters worked hard to receive and breed the local breed of blue cats, which they developed as purebreds under the breeder name, *De Guerveur*. The French Chartreux cats were first recognized as purebreds in 1935; however, the breed stock was too small, and the gene pool

When this cat is in a playful mood, it will use fully extended claws to try to catch anything that moves.

too small to sustain continued pure-breds of the Chartreux breed without the risks of inbreeding.

British shorthair: To remedy this dilemma, potential breed stock was imported from England. Fanciers selected a similar cat breed that had been bred in that country since the end of the nineteenth century. This breed's round head and compact body were a better match for the current breed standards than those of the Chartreux. The leaner bodies of the French cats, which had been crossed with Persian and Russian Blue bloodlines, became less and less popular. As a result, England is credited as being the home and origin of the British shorthair cat. The breed suffered a severe setback in Britain during World War I, and breeders were forced to outcross to other stock in order to increase the gene pool and save the breed. Russian Blues, Burmese, Chartreux, and Persians were used for some of these outcrosses. Today, of course, to maintain its purity, the British shorthair has no allowable outcross breeds.

Breed Recognition in America

Registered shorthairs began to be imported from Britain in the early 1900s, but after arriving in the United States, all were classified as Domestic shorthairs (now called American shorthairs) until the 1950s, when breeders began to take an interest in promoting the American and British varieties as distinct breeds. In 1967 the American Cat Association (ACA) became the first U.S. registry to recognize the British shorthair. At first, only the color blue was recognized; all other colors still had to be registered as Domestics. Not until 1980 did the British shorthair gain separate recognition for championship status in the largest registering body, the Cat Fanciers' Association (CFA). Today, the British shorthair can be registered and shown in all North American associations in approximately 20 different colors. Some associations accept more colors than others.

These associations (listed in the back of this book) not only register cats, they also verify the pedigrees and set rules for breeding and showing. The pedigree of a purebred British shorthair lists several generations of its recorded ancestors. In addition to maintaining stud books, the associations sanction shows, present awards, charter clubs, train judges, and approve breed standards.

British Shorthair Profile

Body: Large to medium and compact or "cobby," with broad, muscular chest, solid shoulders, and level back. Females tend to be less massive than males.

Muscular and solid body type—this is the correct conformation according to the standards for British shorthairs.

Head: Round and massive with a round face set on a short, thick neck. Firm chin and rounded cheeks, with males having larger jowls.

Legs: Short to medium strong legs, straight in the foreleg, well-boned and proportioned to the body.

Paws: Round and firm; five toes in front and four behind.

Tail: Medium length in proportion to the body, thicker at the base, tapering slightly to a rounded tip.

Ears: Medium in size with rounded tips; wide-set and fitting well into the rounded contour of the head.

Eyes: Large, round, wide open, wide-set, and level.

Eye Color: Gold or copper for blue and most coat colors; blue, green, or hazel permitted for certain colors.

Nose: Medium, broad, with a gentle dip when viewed in profile.

Coat: Short, resilient, and dense; fine texture with dense undercoat without being woolly. The top coat must stand out and be evenly colored throughout.

Cause for Disqualification: Oral and dental malformations as well as all other anatomical deviations; defects of the tail, toes, or foot pads; incorrect pad or nose color; green edge around the pupil in copper-colored eyes; weak chin; long or fluffy hair coat.

Source: *The Cat Fanciers' Association, Inc.* Show Standards (1995–1996)

able, loves children, is easy to care for, and loves to be close to humans without clinging, yet it is as devoted as a dog. This cat makes a quiet, even-tempered house companion. Should the need arise, it will assert itself without resorting to tricks. This breed shows no grumpiness or bad humor and holds no grudges. Both sexes generally get along fine with dogs and other house pets when proper introductions are made. In short, this cat is quieter than the average house cat, yet it is more agile and active than the Persian cat, which is known for its passive, gentle nature.

While certain colors, such as the silvers, tend to be more lively and temperamental, the gentlest color variants are

There is nothing like dreaming together!

Character of the British Shorthair

The British shorthair is a particularly strong, high-endurance cat breed. It tends to adapt easily to new situations without giving up its own interests. Given the opportunity from an early age, most will gladly accompany you on all types of errands, visits, and travels. The British shorthair is highly adapt-

usually the "dilutes," such as the blues and creams. British shorthairs are perhaps best described by providing examples of their characteristic behavior:

Traveling: Lady F. was eligible to show off at an international show in Milano. We traveled by airplane, which was no problem for her, because she received attention from the airline personnel. During nights at the hotel,

BKH Lilac: Bavarians Blue, Choco Flight, about 10 months old, male

BKH Creme: Fridolin von Wernerwald, about 12 months old, male

British Shorthair Colors

Apart from the "self" or solid-colored animals, such as the whites, blues, blacks, and creams, the British shorthair comes in an entire painter's palette of variations such as tiger-striped tabbies, smokes, tortoiseshells, calicos, and bicolor (see list, page 11.)

BKH black, Eddy's Dizzy Miss Lizzy, three years old, female

BKH blue, Bavarians Blue, Big William, two years old, male

BKH chocolate, Bavarians Blue, Choco Gipsy, seven months old, female

she slept in her master's bed, and her favorite food was served to her. Although this particular trip was quite tiring for the author, Lady F. returned home without a trace of stress. Indeed, she was her usual quiet, even-tempered self, well-rested and emotionally intact.

Seeking human contact: British shorthairs have a knack for checking out new visitors by intensive scent investigation and, in the course of doing so, getting their share of pats and cuddles. After satisfying this need to check things out, the cat will make a royal retreat, sit back, relax, and watch the goings-on from a respectful distance.

Loving children: Big William lives happily in a family with two children. He particularly enjoys playing with four-year-old Phillip by carefully tossing toy building blocks toward the child

Kittens will find the most original sleeping quarters.

with his little soft paws. When this tom needs a snooze, he chooses the boys' room in order to remain as close to his friends as he can.

Learning: British shorthairs are known for their intelligence, high learning ability, and excellent memory retention. Once they learn how to open a door, they will not forget. My cat, Eliza, wants her time outside on the terrace every morning after breakfast. When I forget to open the door for her to let her out, she proceeds to do it herself. She has also managed to lock me out in the process!

Insisting on routine: Once these cats have adopted a daily routine, they will insist that you consistently provide it. Lady F. insists on her breakfast at a specific early morning hour, and she will remind me of this routine, even if it is Sunday, when I would prefer to sleep in.

Standing their ground: As a rule, adult British shorthairs are courageous and fearless. When precarious situations arise, they seldom panic; they remain levelheaded, coolly assessing the situation. Two-and-a-half-year-old Hunty lives at our friend's home with five-year-old Kalli. One day, unexpected visitors arrived, a man and a big dog. Little Kalli wanted to flee from the invaders, but the adult Hunty prevented a potential chase by picking up Kalli in his jaws in a gentle grip, carrying him to safety, then placing himself in front of the dog, hissing and growling threateningly until the dog owner removed his animal.

British Shorthair Colors

White: Pure white, untipped with yellow. Eye color: deep sapphire blue, gold, or copper.

Black: Jet black to roots, no rusty tinge, no white hair anywhere. Eye color: gold or copper.

Blue: Light to medium blue, lighter shade preferred, very level in color. No tabby markings or white anywhere. Eye color: gold or copper.

Cream: Rich cream, lighter shades preferred, level in color, sound to the roots. No white anywhere. Eye color gold or copper.

Black Smoke: White or pale silver undercoat, deeply tipped with black. Cat in repose appears black. In motion the white or silver undercoat is clearly apparent. Eye color: gold or copper.

Blue Smoke: White or pale silver undercoat, deeply tipped with blue. Cat in repose appears blue. In motion the white or silver undercoat is clearly apparent. Eye color: gold or copper.

Classic tabby pattern: Markings dense, clearly defined, and broad. Legs evenly barred with bracelets coming up to meet the body markings. Tail evenly ringed. Frown marks on forehead form an intricate letter "M." Swirls on cheeks. Vertical lines over back of head extend to shoulder markings, which are in the shape of a butterfly. Back markings consist of a vertical line down the spine from butterfly to tail with a vertical stripe paralleling it on each side. Double vertical rows of buttons on chest and stomach.

Mackeral tabby patterns: Markings dense, clearly defined, and all narrow pencilings. Legs evenly barred with narrow bracelets coming up to meet the body markings. Tail barred. Head barred with an "M" on the forehead. Unbroken lines running back from the eyes. Spine lines run together to form a narrow saddle. Narrow pencilings run around body.

Spotted tabby pattern: Good, clear spotting is essential. The spots can be round, oblong, or rosette-shaped. Color: silver with black spots, brown with black spots, red with deep rich red spots. Any other recognized ground color acceptable with appropriate spotting. Eye color: as for classic tabby.

Silver tabby: Ground color, including lips and chin, pale clear silver. Markings dense black. Eye color: green or hazel.

Red tabby: Ground color red, including lips and chin. Markings deep, rich red. Eye color: gold or copper.

Brown tabby: Ground color brilliant coppery brown. Markings dense black. Eye color: gold or copper.

Blue tabby: Ground color, including lips and chin, pale bluish ivory. Markings a very deep blue affording a good contrast with ground color. Eye color: gold or copper.

Cream tabby: Ground color, including lips and chin, very pale cream. Markings of buff or cream sufficiently darker than the ground color to afford good contrast. Eye color: gold or copper.

Tortoiseshell: Black and rich red to be softly mingled, with both colors clearly defined over the whole animal but without any obvious patches of either color.

Calico: Patches of black and rich red on white, equally balanced. Colors to be brilliant and absolutely free from brindling or tabby markings. The tri-color patching should cover the top of the head, ears, cheeks, back, tail, and part of the flanks. Eye color: gold or copper.

Dilute calico: Patches of blue and cream on white, equally balanced. Colors to be brilliant and absolutely free from brindling or tabby markings. The tri-color patching should cover the top of the head, ears, cheeks, back, tail, and part of the flanks. Eye color: gold or copper.

Blue cream: Blue and cream to be softly mingled, not patched. Eye color: gold or copper.

Bi-color: Black and white, blue and white, red and white, or cream and white. Eye color: gold or copper.

Source: *Cat Fanciers' Association Show Standards*

Buying a British Shorthair

Before you buy, carefully consider how well a cat will fit your lifestyle.

Life with a British Shorthair

A British shorthair adapts easily to a new environment and may, by nature, become extremely attached and dependent on its owner. At the same time, you may find this breed capable of keeping its distance, quite the aristocrat, independent and aloof. The British shorthair is not a lap cat that can be cuddled on command. Quite the contrary—this cat will take the high road and regard you good-naturedly from a distance, but soon it will reconsider its position and voluntarily decide to approach you. At that point, it will expect—even *demand*—intense affection and attention from you.

Before you decide on a British shorthair, answer the following questions:
• Are you or any member of your household allergic to cat hair? If you suffer from asthma or allergies, have a dermatologist test you for sensitivity to cat dander.
• Are you willing to devote 15 to 20 years (average lifespan of a cat) of your life to your pet in terms of daily time and attention?
• Have you considered all of the costs involved in the feeding and maintenance of your cat, including routine vaccinations, annual veterinary checkups, and regular flea control measures?
• What will you do with the cat when you are on vacation, in the hospital, etc? Do you know someone loving and reliable who can care for your pet while you're away?
• Are you willing to live with cat hair and occasional scratches on your furniture, compliments of your new cat companion? Can you live with spilled food crumbs around the cat's feeding area, as well as occasional kitty litter granules tracked out of the litter box? These are just some of the everyday realities of life with a house cat.
• Are you willing to adapt or modify your home and turn it into a "cat safe" environment? Doing so involves removing potential hazards for the cat from your home (see page 25).
• Have you talked with your landlord? Today's housing laws can be complicated, and I strongly suggest that you and your landlord have an agreement before you buy a cat. This will eliminate any potential legal surprises later on.

Where to Get a British Shorthair

Take your time searching for a good British shorthair. Ask for names of responsible breeders in a local, reputable pet supply store, preferably one specializing in cat supplies. Ask your veterinarian, friends, and acquaintances who own purebred cats. More good information sources include cat shows, cat clubs, breeder directories in cat magazines, and professional associations for fanciers of purebred cats (for addresses, see page 62).

Twelve weeks is the minimum age at which a reputable breeder should surrender a kitten to your trust.

This highly prized British shorthair male, called a "tom," rests on his choice of a comfortable watch post.

Finding a Reputable Breeder

If you've decided to buy your British shorthair from a professional breeder, start your search by asking the breeder some of the following questions:

• How long have you bred cats? (Ask for references if the answer is less than five years.)

• Where and how do you raise the kittens? (Kittens should be raised within the family unit and confined to a cage only for short periods when safety considerations prevail.)

• When do you sell your kittens? (The answer should be at the age of at least 12 weeks.)

• Are you a member of a professional breeders' association? (If yes, confirm the answer by contacting the association directly either by phone or in writing.)

• Do you have veterinary health certificates available? (See Health Certificate, page 18.)

More Tips for Recognizing a Reputable Breeder

• A caring breeder will ask you pointed questions about your views and habits on keeping cats. He or she will do this not to be nosy, but rather to make certain that the youngsters will go to good homes with responsible owners.
• With justifiable pride, a reputable breeder should be happy to show you around the cattery. This allows you to observe the environment in which the kitten you are considering buying has been raised. You can also see one or both of the kitten's parents.
• As you tour the facility, note whether the breeder's cats appear fearful and try to avoid you, or whether they purr and rub up against your leg. If properly socialized, kittens should not run and hide as soon as they spot a visitor. Ideally, they should either approach or observe you curiously—even if from a cautious distance—with clear, alert eyes.
• The feline living quarters should be spotlessly clean and have a pleasant or antiseptic odor.

How to Recognize a Healthy Cat

• The eyes are bright, clear, and free of discharge.
• The hair coat is healthy, shiny, and showing no signs of flea dirt, matting, or oiliness.
• The anal area is clean, without signs of residual fecal matter.
• The cat should exhibit a healthy appetite.
• In its familiar surroundings, the cat should appear affectionate and confident rather than timid and fearful.

Kitten or Cat?

Kittens require a lot of time and attention. They are not born knowing how you expect them to behave in your home, so you have to teach them (see HOW-TO: Training Your Kitten, pages 22–23). The advantage of acquiring a kitten is that you can enjoy watching it go through all growth phases, and you can personally influence that process. If you have small children in your house, a grown cat may be a better choice. An adult cat has the stamina to endure turbulent situations without suffering psychological damage, and the experience to get out of a child's way. If you work long hours and have little time to supervise a kitten, an adult cat may also be worth your consideration. Whenever possible, the adult cat of your choice should be less than five years old. It is important to note, however, that older cats may have more difficulties adapting to a new environment.

Male or Female?

Generally, whole male cats, called "toms," are larger and heavier than females. As far as temperament is concerned, you need not worry about any particular differences between males and females. There is, of course, quite a bit of difference in the male and female behaviors as they relate to sexual maturation, such as the rolling behavior of female cats in heat and the territorial spraying of tom cats. Fortunately, these natural but undesirable behaviors can be reduced or eliminated through spaying and neutering (see pages 48–49).

Singles or Doubles?

A cat that receives daily attention and cuddles and whose owner shares activities with it will be quite content as an "only" cat. If, however, space and financial considerations are no obstacle, the acquisition of two cats would definitely be the better solution. The amount of additional work is minimal and despite their aloof, solitary reputations, cats in their domesticated state seek and obviously enjoy the social closeness of their own kind. This closeness stimulates wild, playful battles, often ending in cat-napping and snoozing in favorite locations, sometimes together, sometimes apart. Feline pals also share exchanges of affection, such as licking, grooming, and washing each other. In short, with two cats, there is never a dull moment, not even when all other "human animals" have left the house.

British Shorthairs and Other Cats

Prior to bringing a British shorthair into a house where there is another resident cat, regardless of what breed, be absolutely certain that the new incoming cat is in excellent health before introductions are made. A complete set of vaccinations alone is, unfortunately, not always sufficient insurance. Have the new cat thoroughly examined by a veterinarian. Both cats must be certified free of feline leukemia virus, feline AIDS, and other infectious diseases.

While it may be difficult for two adult cats to adapt to each other, it is not impossible. Pay equal attention to both cats, and remember that the resident cat has primary rights that cannot be avoided. After all, it was there first, and it is being forced to accept the "invading" new cat into its established territory. The process of setting new boundaries and getting close to each other may be a slow one, perhaps lasting hours, days, weeks, or even months, so don't get discouraged.

A kitten is usually more quickly and easily accepted by a resident adult cat

because of the youngster's ignorant, clumsy, and naive behavior. In addition, a kitten often stirs a degree of motherly instincts in an older cat.

Sometimes, a newcomer may be more readily accepted when it carries the owner's scent. To place your scent on the cat, rub its fur and body with an unwashed piece of your personal clothing, especially around the head, paws, and tail, where there are scent

The correct way to pick up a kitten: One hand supports the rear end, while the other firmly grasps the legs between the front paws.

glands. These are the areas that cats sniff first when greeting or identifying one another. Keeping the newcomer isolated for several days in a separate area of the house also allows it to acquire the "house" scent before you introduce it to the resident cat.

British Shorthairs and Other House Pets

Canaries: As a rule, it is not a good idea to keep birds and cats in close proximity as pets, especially unsupervised. First, it could be considered torture to

This play can delight a kitten for hours.

Simply attach a small ball with a string to a basket.

find birds in cages or aviaries beleaguered by cats whose hunting instincts become stimulated whenever the birds move. Secondly, it is noteworthy to remember that birds and felines have quite different sets of natural bacterial growth in their systems, which are not necessarily tolerated by the other species and can become a source of unwanted bacterial infections.

Parrots: While a parrot may initially enjoy a newcomer in the house, watching a cat's playful movements, its sharp and powerful beak is capable of causing serious injuries to a kitten or cat, should the bird ever feel momentarily jealous or threatened.

Hamsters and guinea pigs: According to the laws of nature, remember that these animals look like lunch or dinner in the eyes of our little home tigers. They should *never* be left unsupervised in the company of cats. However, pets of different species, even predator and prey, can achieve a peaceful coexistence as long as separate quarters are always maintained.

Aquarium: Fish provide welcome entertainment for a cat's life; in fact, your cat may spend hours watching the underwater show with fascination. However, it is essential to cover the aquarium with a sturdy hood to safeguard the fish from unexpected fishing and swimming expeditions by your feline.

Dogs: Provided the dog has learned to recognize cats as friends and has not had early experiences and encouragement in chasing cats, few problems can be expected among cohabiting felines and canines. The simplest way to carry out the introduction is to "present" the kitten to the dog as you would a gift. Keep the dog on a leash initially, just in case it is tempted to chase the cat. Also, the kitten needs to have had some time to get acclimated to the new home before you can present it to the dog. This way, it will feel more comfortable with its new environment and more trusting and safe with its owners when it is faced with the dog. The kitten will, then, transfer that trusting relationship to the dog. For example, when the kitten is relaxed enough to stretch out comfortably on your lap, it is time to let the dog take a careful sniff. Supervise their contact for awhile, as it may take time for natural barriers of fear and mistrust to vanish. If you exercise some caution and sensitivity, your dog and cat should soon become bonded friends.

Rabbits: One more example of unusual friendships to close this chapter: The British shorthair tom "Nicky," a strong and youthful specimen of my breeding stock, shared his new home with a rabbit. For the first year, it was the rabbit that was the master in all matter of play; however, little by little, our Nicky started to learn how to get even by using what he learned from Mr. Long-Ears. Yet the two remained friends through games and battles. Nicky would sit patiently and wait longingly until the bunny cage was opened and his friend was released for play and companionship. Two years later, when Mr. Long-Ears died, Nicky mourned so much that he was given a new long-eared friend as a playmate. The new duo live together as happily and uncomplicated as the previous friends.

British Shorthairs and Children

Cats are a natural source of happiness and serenity for adults; the same is true for children. Research has clearly established that the companionship of cats is especially beneficial for sensitive children and therapeutic for those with some psychological problems.

Because of the particularly even temper and gentle nature of the British shorthairs, their relationships with children commonly turn out to be inseparable. This breed of cat is ready to participate in any activity while it is in the mood to play, yet it will let you know in no uncertain terms when it wants to be left undisturbed.

Children must be taught how to properly hold and handle cats because their unintentional roughness can injure

"Oops, didn't I just hear something stir in the bushes?"

a kitten or result in the child being clawed by a defensive feline. Always supervise contact among cats and kids, especially very young children. Let the child know that a cat is not a toy, but a living creature with feelings and a will of its own. While it's important to teach a child how to care for a cat, under no circumstances should a child be expected to take full responsibility, without adult supervision, for the maintenance of a cat or any other animal.

When a Baby Is Expected

A woman who has a cat as a house-mate need only take a few hygienic precautions during pregnancy (see toxoplasmosis, page 44). The cat can stay but leaving a newborn baby alone in a room with a cat is not recom-mended. This is because an infant's cries and jerky motions may startle or frighten a curious cat, resulting in an accidental scratching injury. To avoid potential mishaps, it is simply safer to supervise all contact between infant and cat for awhile. Put a screen door on the nursery, if necessary, or place a mesh tent, available at baby supply stores, over the baby's crib to keep the cat away from the baby.

Purchase Contracts and Other Papers

In the eyes of the law, a cat is a material possession. As such, a cat should come with a sales contract, as with any other material purchase. This helps protect the seller's and the buyer's rights. The following items should be part of a sales contract:
- Names and addresses of seller and buyer
- Name of the cat and the breeder
- Name of the cat's parents
- Birthdate of the cat
- Breed
- Color
- Pedigree number
- Purchase price

In addition, the seller may stipulate whether the cat can be used for breeding purposes or whether it must be spayed or neutered. The seller has the right to withhold registration papers until the buyer furnishes proof that the cat has been altered so that it cannot reproduce.

Pedigree

The breeder is also responsible for furnishing correct pedigree information. While this document's purpose is to list all known ancestors of both the dam and the sire, usually only four or five generations are required to be given on the papers. The cat association(s) in which the breeder has registered the litter is charged with keeping the stud books on recognized breeds and with verifying pedigrees.

Health Certificate

Any reputable breeder will furnish the buyer with the kitten's veterinary health certificate, confirming which vaccina-tions have been given and which ones, if any, are due. A kitten should have had at least two sets of shots in its young life to prevent feline distemper and assorted upper respiratory diseases (see Vaccinations Schedule, page 43.)

You should have the kitten examined by your own veterinarian within a week of purchase to be certain that it is healthy and free of parasites. In case problems arise, your sales contract should clearly stipulate the terms of a return agreement.

Basic Necessities

By the time the new family member arrives, all essential supplies should already be assembled in their proper places. The basic necessities are as follows:

Food: Discuss the best choice of food with your breeder or veterinarian prior to bringing home your new cat. Commercial cat foods are designed to meet the needs of a cat's various life stages—kitten, adult maintenance, pregnant, and lactating. For a kitten, select an appropriate brand formulated with the extra protein and nutrients kittens need for healthy growth.

Food and water bowls: Choose from your existing plates and bowls, as long as the containers are stable and easily sanitized, or you can find a large assortment of food bowls in any pet shop. Glass, porcelain, or glazed, lead-free pottery are preferable to plastic as some cats develop allergies to plastic materials.

Litter box: Again, any pet shop has a variety of litter boxes, from the plain, open tub types to the fancy ones with covers or pull-out trays for easy cleaning. Always provide one litter box per cat in the household.

Kitty litter: Clumping litter varieties are a good choice because they allow for excellent hygiene and odor control. The material is designed to clump wherever it gets wet, making it easy for you to scoop out the urine wastes along with the solid fecal matter. Some cats strongly dislike perfumed litter varieties. For these finicky types, plain clay litter is a better choice. Also, unless the product claims to be flushable, soiled litter should be put in the trash, never in the toilet.

Scoop: This tool is optional but useful for removing solid wastes from the litter box. Choose one with holes or slots so that dry, clean litter falls through into the litter box, leaving behind only the wastes.

Pet carrier: This item is essential for safe transport to the veterinarian or for vacation travel. Select a sturdy, plastic pet kennel (see drawing, page 42).

Cat bed or blanket: Most cats gladly accept a clean, cozy blanket or a small, round bed to curl up in. Pet stores offer a variety of styles, colors, and types of cat beds. Select something that can be laundered easily.

Scratching post and toys: See HOW-TO: Choosing the Right Activities for Your Cat, pages 34–35.

Brushes, combs: See HOW-TO: Grooming Your British Shorthair, pages 26–27.

Important: Remove all potential danger sources from your home and garden. (For tips, see pages 25.)

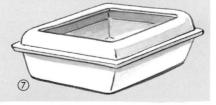

Pet shops offer a myriad of supplies and toys. Here are a few examples:
① Small ball with an attached bell
② Cuddle blankets
③ Rubber hedgehog
④, ⑤ Rattles
⑥ Toy mouse
⑦ Litter box

Getting Used to the New Home and Daily Life

Eddy's Red Hazel, an adult female red British shorthair. The British shorthair cat appears in several recognized colors.

The day you bring your British short-hair kitten home, try to be available for an extended weekend dedicated to it. When you go to the breeder to pick up your kitten, take with you the blanket or pillow you bought for your new friend. Ask the breeder to rub the blanket against the bodies of the kitten's mother and siblings to take on the familiar scent. Then add your own scent to theirs. This may help make your kitten's adaptation to its new home less stressful.

Transport

On the way home, keep your new cat inside a transport basket or plastic kennel and secure the cat carrier in the seat with the seatbelt. Drive slowly and keep the cat away from any drafts.

First Days and Nights

After you reach home, place the cat carrier next to the kitten's litter box. Open the carrier and talk to the kitten calmly and reassuringly. Coax it out of its cage and maneuver it gently toward the litter box. Allow the kitten to explore and sniff its new surroundings undisturbed for a few minutes. Show the cat where its food and water bowls are, but don't expect it to eat right away. The cat will probably sniff around the food bowl first and wait to eat later, when it feels more relaxed. After the kitten eats its first meal or two, continue the orientation by taking it back to the litter box, placing it gently in the box, and reaffirming its comfort with quiet, reassuring talk. Soon the little animal will accept its new home. Try to plan this adaptational time to be as calm and stress-free as possible. Do not allow guests and friends to disturb this process in order to create a much stronger basis for the cat's positive adjustment and development.

Sleeping Quarters

A new home brings about so many new impressions, a tiring affair for your little kitten. Now it needs a rest, and a place to sleep. You might want to place the original blanket, which you had prepared for the trip home, in a quiet, warm place, but do not assume the kitten will automatically accept this idea and sleep where you intend it to. Instead, it may choose to curl up in a completely different location.

If you do not want your kitten to sleep with you, begin teaching it to stay off your bed from the first day. This means keeping the door to your bedroom shut. If you allow the kitten to sleep on your bed once, it may be quite difficult (and unfair) to convince it to sleep elsewhere. Most adult British shorthairs prefer not to seek their nest under your bedcovers—with their dense fur, they simply get too hot. These cats prefer sleeping on top of the blankets or at the end of the bed.

Yes, you can train cals! If you do not want your kitten to pick up bad habits such as clawing or climbing the drapes, you must begin training it early. When your kitten misbehaves, yell *"No!"* in a sharp tone and clap your hands loudly. Be consistent and firm. Never strike the kitten with your hand or with any object.

If you love your curtains, you need to train your kitten right.

HOW-TO:
Training Your Kitten

Cats are highly individual, strong-willed creatures. Although they can be trained, the way you train them differs greatly from the way you would train a dog. If you begin training early, and patiently communicate to your kitten from the outset how you expect it to behave in your home, you will end up with a well-behaved cat companion.

Important Training Tips
• Be calm and deliberate when training your kitten.
• Teach a *no* command and reinforce by adding a hissing sound like "Pssst!" or a loud clapping of hands. These sounds are extremely unpleasant for feline ears.
• Follow any "done deed" on the spot with your positive or negative reaction—even a few minutes later your cat can no

1| *British shorthairs love to learn and usually adapt quickly to being harnessed for a walk.*

longer make the connection to your praise or scolding.
• Use the same word each time for any meaningful command. Make it a short word.
• Be consistent. Do not give permission today for something you won't allow tomorrow.
• Never hit a cat! Once beaten, a cat will respond to people with fear and aggression.

Leash Training Your Cat
Drawing 1
As a rule, cats do not take naturally to walking on a leash. Leash training, however, is not difficult and is, in fact, a useful pursuit. When you travel by car, for example, you can let your cat out on a harness and leash to stretch its legs without fear of it escaping. It's important to begin leash training as early as possible.

How to Begin
Placing the harness on the kitten for the first time should be done in a mode of playfulness:
• Place the kitten on your lap and attach the harness while you reassure it quietly and lovingly.
• Offer a treat and some praise. Place the kitten gently on the floor.
• Keep the leash short and allow the kitten to walk where it wants as you follow, holding the lead.
• After a few minutes, pick up the kitten and reward with another treat.
• Remove the harness and lavish more praise on the student.

Follow-up Training Sessions
Repeat the above procedure, gradually extending the length of

2| *A cat should not pay attention to a table set for a meal.*

time on the leash. When the cat is comfortable on the leash inside, you can take it outside for short walks in a quiet area. Never tie up your cat or leave it unsupervised on a leash, as it can become entangled or accidentally hang itself.

Begging at the Table
Drawing 2
Cats do not normally beg for food unless someone has fed them scraps from the dinner table,. To prevent begging, simply feed your cat its own food in its own place, away from the kitchen table. If you must offer table scraps, put them in the cat's bowl.

Scratching Furniture and Upholstery
Drawing 3
Cats have an innate need to sharpen their claws. Sharp claws are essential for survival, for climbing trees, for marking territory, for catching prey, and for fighting feline battles. Of course, you do not want your cat to exer-

cise this natural behavior on your favorite overstuffed armchair, so you will have to provide it with a scratching post of its own.

In case your newly obtained friend proceeds straight for your armchair, with claws poised, ready to scratch, pronounce your loudest, clearest *"No!"* and firmly remove the attacker from the crime scene. Carry the cat to the scratching post, place its paws on the post, and move them in a scratching motion. You will have better success if you place the scratching post in the room where you spend most of your time.

Correcting Misbehavior
Drawing 4

Following are some additional tips for those occasions when your kitten is about to commit some misdeed:

• First, call out your sharpest *"No!"* or *"Down!"* Never use your cat's name in conjunction with negative commands, as this will discourage it from coming to you when called.

• In conjunction with a negative command, you can shoot a jet of clean water from a water pistol or a plant spray bottle. The clatter of a metallic chain thrown on the floor or the rattle of a newspaper slapped against a couch cushion at the moment you yell *"No!"* often works wonders. Your success depends on the element of surprise and on your kitten *not* discovering the source of the disturbance.

• Remember, too, your success depends on you catching the little sinner "in the act" and quickly administering the repri-

mand right then, *not* minutes or hours after the fact when the cat can no longer associate your wrath with its wrongdoing.

Litter Box Training
Kittens learn from their mothers how to use the litter box or eliminate outside the nest. When you bring home your kitten, simply reinforce this learned behavior by showing the kitten where to find the litter pan. The rest will come naturally.

The litter box must be kept immaculately clean, or the cat, being a naturally fastidious crea-

3| The best place for a scratch board is right next to the sofa.

ture, may refuse to use it. Do not use pungent chemicals or bleach for cleaning; a little vinegar in the water will do.

Place the litter box is a quiet place, out of the way of foot traffic and well protected from drafts and noise. Your bathroom or an extra guest bathroom are good choices.

Sudden Housesoiling
If the kitten suddenly soils an area outside the litter box, rule out physical or medical causes first, before assuming that the problem is psychological. If you notice it making frequent visits to the litter box, straining to urinate, or passing blood-tinged urine, suspect a lower urinary tract disorder and seek veterinary help immediately. Your cat may have tiny mineral crystals irritating or blocking its urethra, a condition that is potentially life threatening (see FLUTD, page 44).

4| Pin curtains high and tie drapery cords out of reach.

After ruling out medical causes, evaluate recent changes in the cat's life. Sometimes, cats will resort to housesoiling if they don't like the litter box location or the litter box filler. Experiment with moving the box to a different location or trying different types of litter to determine the cat's preferences.

How to Pick up a Kitten

When picking up your new kitten, do not grab it under the belly. A kitten feels safer and more comfortable when you pick it up by placing one hand flat under its rear end while placing your other hand between the front legs (see drawing, page 20).

A Home Fit for a Cat

You may need to rearrange your home in certain ways to fit the needs of a cat, if you want it to feel safe and well-adjusted. This breed of cat does not prefer a large house to a small apartment. On the contrary, the typical British shorthair would choose a one-room studio to a mansion, if living in a studio meant that it would get more attention.

Where to place the cat's belongings: Do not place food bowls or sleeping quarters next to the kitty toilet. The cat will either not accept this arrangement, or problems will develop quickly. Separate places for feeding, eliminating, and sleeping are essential. Choose quiet areas that can give your cat a sense of privacy.

Curtains: Floor-length curtains are sure to present irresistible temptations to the climbing instincts of a kitten. If you tie up your curtains and place them out of reach for a few weeks or months you will have won a battle without a fight.

Upholstery: You will also win a battle without a fight if, during the initial training phase, you cover your upholstery with protective blankets. Then, as you place scratch boards, sisal mats, or scratching posts in strategic locations, the kitten should soon adopt these, instead of your furniture, as favorite places to sharpen claws.

Carpeting: If you are planning to recarpet your home, consider the needs of your feline companion: A thick pile carpet is preferable to a closely woven style because the cat's claws get stuck in loops and weaves of carpet threads. Also, consider a natural fiber carpet over a material that accumulates static energy. In general, your new carpet should be safe as long as you offer sufficient scratching post opportunities.

Scratching post: Solid, stable scratching posts and climbing trees are a must in your cat's household. There are no limits to your creative fancy. Pet shops carry innumerable models and modules, that you can combine according to the size and decor of your apartment or house. If you want to build your own model, see pages 34–35.

Cat grass: Cats love to nibble grass; it seems to act as a natural purgative for cleaning swallowed hair out of the digestive system. You can purchase kitty greenery from pet shops, or sow your own grass seed in a flowerpot. When ready to "harvest," place the cat grass near the cat's food bowl; do not place it near your other houseplants. In addition to cat grass, you may want to grow some catnip, a member of the mint family that causes some cats to roll and play ecstatically.

Window perch: These perches that attach easily to the windowsill allow indoor cats to have a view to the outside world. A bird feeder in close proximity outside will provide your cat with ample entertainment. Just make sure all window screens are sturdy and secure enough to hold your cat's weight when pressed against them.

Other considerations: Your living quarters represent your cat's territory. If you tend to move your furniture a lot, this will disturb your cat's sense of territory and possibly lead to behavior problems. Under natural conditions, a cat surveys its territory on daily outings. For the indoor cat, each detail of your living

When the weather is hot, cats like to dream in a cool, shady spot.

room is part of this specific territorial map. Each piece of furniture is a familiar detail to your cat. When you move everything around, your cat's territory becomes confusing, and sensitive animals may respond with undesirable behaviors.

Sources of Danger in House and Garden

To make your home safe for a cat, do the same things you would do to make it child-safe. Following are some suggestions:

Bathroom: To prevent accidental drowning, keep the door to your bathroom closed and toilet lids down.

Chemicals, cleaning agents, and medicines: Keep all types of household cleaners and laundry detergents in closed cabinets.

Electrical cords: Cover exposed extension cords and other electrical cables with carpeting, matting, or PVC piping.

Plants: Remove poisonous plants from the home. Some examples are: orchids, ivy, poinsettia, African violets, dieffenbachia, narcissus, azaleas, and lily of the valley. For a complete list of plants toxic to cats, call the National Animal Poison Control Information Center at (800) 548-2423. A small fee is charged.

Laundry machines: Keep washer and dryer doors closed at all times. Make it a habit to check both the dryer and washer before you start them.

Stovetops and other fire or hot spots: Do not leave any source of fire or heat unattended when you are raising a kitten. Screen fireplaces. Unplug small appliances when not in use.

HOW-TO: Grooming Your British Shorthair

The coat of a British shorthair consists of three layers: the longer guard hairs, the softer awn hairs, and the down or wool hairs. Compared to longhaired cats, the British shorthair's fur is easy to maintain. Combing and brushing every other week is sufficient. Brushing this type of cat more often may stimulate hair growth, and your cat will begin to shed increasingly because its natural hair growth pattern has been disturbed.

Combing
Drawing 1 and 2

Place your cat on your lap and begin combing at the head and continue all the way to the tail. Comb through all furry parts once or twice. Then, turn the cat over on its back, and comb under its chin and through the belly hair.

A metal comb with rounded teeth is the most useful type. Get one with medium- or wide-spaced, short teeth.

A flea comb is useful when you suspect fleas or other external parasites are inhabiting your cat's fur. The fine, closely spaced teeth trap the insects and flea dirt as you comb. To drown fleas caught in the teeth, simply dip the comb in a nearby pan of water.

Brushes
To brush your cat, proceed exactly as you did for combing, except brush in the opposite direction, against the direction of natural hair growth, in order to make the hair coat of a British shorthair "stand out." This allows the dense undercoat to fully develop.

Natural bristle brushes are much kinder to your cat's skin and fur than metal or plastic brushes.

Shedding
British shorthairs shed more hair during the fall and spring seasons. During this time, you should comb and brush the cat weekly. If you notice your cat shedding heavily for a prolonged period or constantly, consult a veterinarian. Stress, hormonal imbalances, or nutritional problems can wreak havoc with the coat.

Dandruff can also be caused by stress or nutritional imbalances. If you suspect the problem may be stress related, find the origin and remove the cause. If you suspect the problem may be food related, change to a higher-quality brand. Consult your veterinarian if the problem worsens or continues. To remove the excess dander, bathe and brush your cat.

Greasy Hair Coat
Oily hair and increased shedding can also be caused by stress or nutritional factors. Older cats sometimes develop an oily coat because their decreasing flexibility makes them less able to do a good job of self-grooming. If this is the case, you need to help your cat by grooming it more often. An occasional bath is helpful,

2| *Comb from the head toward the tail and brush in the opposite direction.*

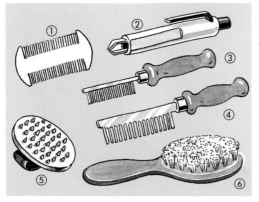

1| *Essential grooming tools include:*
① *Double-sided flea comb*
② *Tick remover*
③ *Fine-toothed metal comb*
④ *Wide-toothed metal comb*
⑤ *Rubber curry comb*
⑥ *Natural bristle brush*

but bathing too frequently can interfere with the natural coat condition and lead to dry skin problems.

Stud Tail

This problem affects some toms of this breed. The condition is hormonally induced by over-productive sebaceous glands at the tail base. The overactive glands contribute to matted, oily hair in this area. The condition is usually associated with puberty and is controlled by neutering. To remedy, wash the area with a cat-safe shampoo, being careful to rinse out all traces of soap.

Cleaning the Eyes
Drawing 3

A minimal amount of secretion at the corners of the eyes is normal. To remove, use a clean cotton ball or tissue and gently wipe toward the nose. If the tearing seems excessive, consult a veterinarian—your cat may have an eye infection or an injury to the cornea that requires treatment.

Cleaning the Ears
Drawing 4

The inside of the ears should be clean and pink; however, some cats go through phases when they produce more ear wax than normal. Should you notice this, use a clean cotton ball and wipe firmly but gently by pressing the tip of your finger against the hollow space of the ear flap. Do not use force and *never* use Q-tips: Poking anything into the ear canal can cause serious damage to the sensitive struc-

3 | *Remove secretions from the corners of the eyes by using a clean tissue and gently wiping toward the nose.*

4 | *Use a cotton ball and the pressure of your fingertip to clean the inside of your cat's ear flaps.*

tures of the inner ear. If the ear wax is excessive, has a fruity odor, or appears brown and crusty, or if you notice the cat shaking its head and scratching its ears, consult a veterinarian. Ear mites or other infections may be the culprit (see page 48). Your veterinarian can also prescribe prophylactic ear drops that are useful for routine ear care.

Dental Care

To reduce the accumulation of dental tartar (brownish deposits at the base of the teeth), feed your cat dry food and brush its teeth once or twice a week. The hard chewing action required with dry food helps scour the teeth clean. Also, if you start when your cat is a kitten, you can teach it to tolerate having its teeth brushed but every year or two, your cat will still need a professional dental cleaning at the veterinarian's office.

Brushing Teeth

At a pet shop, purchase a small, soft-bristle pet toothbrush and toothpaste designed specifically for cats. Do not use human tooth-paste, as this can burn the throat and cause stomach upset. To accustom your cat to having its teeth brushed, start by wrapping your finger in gauze and dipping it in something tasty, such as tuna juice. Gently rub a few teeth. Praise the cat when it cooperates. With each session, rub a few more teeth until you're able to do all at one time. By now, the cat should accept the toothbrush without much fuss. The enzymatic action of the pet toothpaste cleans the teeth and requires no rinsing. Also, it is generally not necessary to clean the inside of the teeth.

Inflamed gums, called *gingivitis,* appear reddish and swollen and can lead to tooth loss or serious infections if left untreated. Bad breath is a common sign of gingivitis and requires veterinary attention to determine the cause and best course of treatment.

Doors: Doors are danger spots for kittens, especially ones that shut forcefully or automatically. Remember to close doors carefully while your kitten is young—their paws have a way of getting in the openings at the wrong time.

Balconies and open windows: Secure these potential hazards by screening with strong, sturdy wire or nylon mesh to prevent the cat from falling or jumping.

Garden ponds and swimming pools: Secure the circumference of a steep-sided garden pond or swimming pool either with netting or electrified fencing.

Toys: Supervise all play with fishing pole-type toys that have feather or sparkler lures attached to the end of a dangling string. Store these toys safely in a closet when not in use. Strings, threads, yarns, and cords can result in tragic strangulation, or if swallowed, in a potentially life-threatening intestinal blockage called *string enteritis.* Watch out for toys with tied-on bells and button eyes; if these come loose, they can be easily swallowed, causing choking or an obstruction.

A child's room offers a variety of opportunities for play.

Traveling with Your British Shorthair

British shorthair cats usually make good travelers. The earlier you get your kitten accustomed to traveling, the fewer problems you will encounter when the cat gets older. Take along enough of your cat's regular food on your trip, and don't forget the cat harness, food bowls, litter box, kitty litter, and the poop scoop.

If you will be starting your trip early in the morning, feed your cat the last meal on the evening prior to your departure. Water need not be restricted, but an empty stomach travels lighter.

If you're traveling to a foreign country, determine in advance what vaccination and health certificates you will need for your cat. Arrange to get all this information at least five or six weeks prior to your intended departure date.

Traveling by Car

Secure the cat in a cat carrier during the ride. If you are traveling far, you will need to take a break every few hours, offer your passenger water, and place the litter box close to the cat in case it is time for a little relief.

If warm temperatures prevail, you must park the car in a shady spot, and *never* leave the cat unattended in a parked car, not even with the windows cracked.

Traveling by Plane

Some airlines allow you to travel with your cat in the passenger section of the plane, but to do so, you must make arrangements well in advance. To carry a cat onboard, you will need an airline-regulation cat carrier that fits under a seat. If you have more than one cat to transport, or if you fail to make the appropriate preparations, the animal must be shipped in the cargo section of

British shorthairs bond quickly and inseparably with children.

the plane. The latter is not only expensive, but is truly stressful and risky for your pets. The cargo section of an airplane is pressurized and temperature controlled while in the air, but not while on the ground. This means that, while the plane is loading or waiting for take-off, your cat could be experiencing uncomfortable—even dangerous—fluctuations in temperature. To reduce the risk, avoid flying with your cat in extremely hot or cold weather, and make sure the plane's pilot knows that an animal is in the cargo hold.

Boarding

Take time to find and evaluate the available boarding facilities in your area. If your veterinarian offers boarding services, you will have the peace of mind knowing that your cat is in an expert's care, should it become ill while

you're away. If you plan to use a boarding kennel, visit the facility first and make sure that it is clean. Any reputable facility will require proof of vaccinations before accepting your cat.

Staying in Your Home

This solution is definitely my choice of cat care options, because the animal stays in a familiar environment, and therefore experiences less stress. Of course, this option is acceptable only if you know a reliable person who is able and willing to take care of your pet while you're away, perhaps another cat owner with whom you can exchange cat care obligations. A more expensive alternative is to hire the services of a professional pet sitter who specializes in the care and husbandry of pets in their homes. Most urban areas list them in the yellow pages.

Interpreting Feline Behavior

British shorthairs have neither lost nor forgotten their ancestors' heritage. Mama cat teaches her children early how to behave and how to relate to each other. While cats are, by nature, solitary creatures, we know that they adapt well to living in groups, however, the more cats you keep in a confined area, the more problems you are likely to have.

Marking

Rubbing: Your cat's territory includes your apartment, your furniture and, yes, you. A cat marks its territory by rubbing its head or hindquarters against objects. When your cat rubs against your legs, it is not merely showing affection; it is actually marking you as its property. But watch out when you're dealing with an unaltered tom cat! On occasion, he will so delight in his heady fervor of marking that he may spray (see below).

Scratching: Scratching serves a dual purpose for marking territory, in addition to sharpening the claws. Both rubbing and scratching behavior allows the release of scent from the many scent glands that are distributed over a cat's body—at the temples, the corners of the mouth, the base of the tail, and in the pads of the front paws. The deposit of this scent tells a cat, "I was here." Of course, humans fail to read these signs because we cannot smell them, but other cats can.

Spraying: Unlike the scent left by rubbing and scratching, the scent of spraying is quite offensive to human noses. This natural but undesirable marking behavior is a release of concentrated urine. Typically, the cat stands and squirts a stream of pungent urine on a wall or vertical surface.

Although it is more common for male cats to spray, both sexes will spray if engaged in a dispute over dominance or territory. Some females in heat spray. In feline language, urine spraying attracts mates and discourages territorial rivals. Once spraying becomes an established habit, it is difficult to break. Fortunately, spraying can be reduced or eliminated by neutering males and spaying females before they ever start the habit.

Body Language

Tail: Your cat shows it is happy to see you when it approaches with ears pricked forward and tail held high. However, when you see the tip of the tail vibrating, watch out! This cat is at the end of its patience and wants to be left alone. The last stage before final attack is characterized by a cat's tail beating heavily, accompanied by an angry stance and drawling meow sounds.

Back arching: The angry stance that signals an impending attack is an arched, bristled back. At the same time, the cat flattens the ears backwards and utters threatening meows and growls.

Flehmen response: Once a cat has imprinted its scent on an object, other cats will "read" the messages with great interest. To do so, a cat opens the mouth slightly and curls back the upper lip in a snarl. This behavior, known as the *flehmen response*, increases air contact over the mucosal surfaces and optimizes the scent experience. Every "word of the message" can thus be deciphered.

Grooming behavior: You will notice that your cat will groom itself as soon as you stop petting it. Licking its body in long strokes shows you how content and happy your cat feels. This grooming behavior also follows after feeding.

Kneading: Kittens are born with this instinctive behavior. By kneading their mother's mammary glands with their paws, they stimulate the milk flow from the nipples. Many cats retain this behavior into adulthood and will knead their owners' laps with claws extended when they feel happy and secure. If your cat does this, you can still enjoy having your cat in your lap by spreading a blanket over your lap to protect your clothes and skin.

Rolling: When your cat rolls on its back in front of you, purring, and turning its head languidly from side to side, it is expressing security, trust, and deep contentment. This action also may be interpreted as an invitation to scratch the belly, but beware! Some cats have ticklish bellies and will sink their claws into your hand.

Lifting paws: When your cat lifts its paw and flattens its ears, this is a subtle request to "Please leave me alone."

"Covering" food: On occasion, you may observe your cat sniffing that favorite brand of food in its bowl, then scratching and pretending to cover the food with invisible ground. The cat will walk away, only to return later to the "covered" food and eat it with the usual delight. Domestic felines have retained this ancient survival tactic from their wild ancestors, who routinely covered some of their food to provide reserves in times of need.

Vocal Language

Meow sounds: Soon you will learn to understand a mere meow from meeoow! and all of its variations. One intonation of meow means "hello," another is an invitation to play, while still another, accompanied by purring and running ahead of you to the kitchen, obviously means that it is time to feed the baby.

Chattering: This peculiar clicking and gurgling sound indicates excitement over sightings of birds or a buzzing fly through a windowpane.

Growling: This sound does not necessarily mean that your cat is ready to attack. It is more often a warning that the cat does not want to be

Testing their strength is part of kitten play. "I am stronger than you are."

If it moves it must be pursued

and caught.

approached. For example, our Lady F. might be lying serenely and happily in a quiet place when her brood approaches. Her deep growling sounds tell her offspring to leave Mom in peace. Growling is also ritual behavior during battles among territorial rivals and mating competitors.

Purring: This well-known, beloved sound usually expresses contentment. Cats also use purring to invite you to play or to greet you and say, "Cuddle me, and I'll be yours." However, cats also purr when they are sick. In my vocabulary, this usage means that the animal is saying, "Help," and is attempting to calm itself in the process.

Feline Ranking Order

Several cats living together in a group develop an internal ranking order. Usually, one or two top cats

enjoy preferential status. Whenever our Lady F. receives a young live-in mate, she changes her ladylikeness to that of a boss. First, she goes nose to nose in a rather haughty manner and then proceeds to sniff the rear end of the young intruder. However, when the little fuzzball wants to do the same, it gets put in its place with determined hissing language informing it of its low ranking. This is the feline way of establishing house order. Of course, this does not mean that Lady F. wants nothing to do with the lower ranks. On the contrary, she does, but she first has to establish that she is "top cat." After she has had a snooze, she will choose an appropriate moment to tell the young underlings that she is now ready to have fun. With loud meows she excites their playfulness, and off they go on a wild chase through the house.

The game starts over again.

Your Cat's Senses

Eyes

Cats have excellent vision. Their eyes adapt to varying degrees of light by adjusting the pupil's width. In dim light, their pupils are large and round; in sunlight, they are as thin as slits. However, in pitch-darkness, there is no visibility, even for cats. Unlike dogs, cats can distinguish between such colors as black, white, and red.

Ears

Cats have a highly developed auditory system. They register even the minutest sounds. Even while sleeping, a cat will not miss a passing mouse.

Sensory Hairs

The whiskers, found around the mouth and above the eyes, are special hairs so sensitive to touch that even a blind cat can orient itself in its own territory. Cats also have special sensory hairs on the paws. Even kittens can use the sensitivity of their whiskers to check narrow openings for passage.

Nose

Because of the small size of the feline nose, cats do not possess as good a sense of smell as dogs. Nevertheless, cats still have a remarkably good sense of smell and show it by recognizing the scent profile of just about any human or animal in their territory.

Taste

Tiny taste buds cover the cat's tongue. Contrary to common belief, however, cats are not gourmet tasters, their taste computer is programmed by habit and by routine encounters with foods and food textures.

HOW-TO: Choosing the Right Activities for Your Cat

Toys belong in every cat household, especially if the cat spends a lot of time alone while its owner works outside of the house. If this is true in your case, prepare to spend quality time with your cat as soon as you come home.

The Right Toys

The assortment of toys for fitness training range from solid rubber balls and catnip mice to toy fishing poles and rings. Pet stores stock a multitude of toys, but a typical household can produce its own variety of playthings for cats, such as cardboard rolls, paper balls, socks stuffed with catnip, empty spools of thread (no threaded spools, please!), and much more.

When choosing a cat toy, the number one consideration is safety. Following are some unsafe items to avoid:
- bells
- buttons
- plastic eyes
- rubber bands
- bread wrapper ties
- paper clips
- small pieces of soft rubber
- wadded balls of newspaper or aluminum foil.

Such small items may be easily swallowed or chewed off and become lodged in the intestinal tract, where they can cause serious problems.

Cardboard Box House
Drawing 1

Large cartons transform easily into fun playhouses. Cut several holes in the sides of the carton. The holes should be large enough for your cat to move comfortably in and out. Then turn the box upside down. You will soon find your cat spending hours moving in and out, chasing from one hole through the next to the top and out the side again.

Catnip Euphoria

You can offer your cat its "opium" in the form of catnip. This natural herb gives some cats a temporary "high," but it's harmless and nonaddictive. In fact, catnip appears to calm the senses and promote a sense of well-being in cats. Pet stores sell the dried chopped leaves, which you can use to make your own catnip-stuffed toys. Or, you can buy an array of ready-made catnip mice and sacks. Dried catnip leaves are also useful for training purposes: Rub the herbal essence over the surface of a new scratching post or on the desired sleeping quarters to entice your cat to accept them more quickly.

Building a Scratching Post
Drawing 2

For the average handyman, a scratching post is an easy home project. Just follow some of these tips:

Buy the pole—3.9 × 3.9 inches (10 × 10 cm)—and have the edges rounded off by a carpenter.
- Buy two or more boards for shelves—13.8 × 19.7 inches (35 × 50 cm) and 10 inches (2. 5 cm) thick.
- In each board, cut a hole from the edge of the narrow end (see Drawing 4). Once the rope is strung around the pole, this space will be filled.
- Next, attach an angle iron between post and board. There should be two screw holes in each angle and the length should be a minimum of 7.9 inches (20 cm).
- Now, place the board over the pole and fasten the screws to fix the boards at the right height. Provide at least one board at about the middle height and one way up on the top.

1⌋ Cardboard house: You can create a playhouse for your cats quickly and easily. They will delight in climbing in and out for hours.

34

Stabilizing the post: Install angle irons at both ends by fastening screws in the floor and ceiling (Drawing #2). You can also use aluminum fittings by drilling holes in premeasured places.

Covering the post with rope: Now that the structure is finished, all that is left to do is to wind sisal rope around the entire length of the "tree." You can find the right rope in pet supply stores, upholstery shops, or hardware stores.

You will need approximately 100 inches (254 cm) of rope for an eight-foot high (2.44 m) pole.

Add an additional 10 percent length, because the rope is going to be quite compressed by pulling and pushing it tightly.

Fix the rope with hooks approximately each tenth round of winding. Just make sure that the hooks are nailed in deep and tight so that no injuries can occur later.

Hint: Moisten the rope slightly before you wrap it around the pole. This will tighten the fit when the rope dries and it will provide stronger resistance to the forthcoming tortures by cat claws.

Additional Points to Keep in Mind as You Build
• The post must be solid and stable. Also, the taller the better, and up to the ceiling is best.
• One long side of the post should remain uninterrupted and smooth without protruding boards or steps. This allows a cat to climb up the post in one smooth run.

• Plan a high location for a preferably padded shelf from which your cat will enjoy an unrivaled view. If desired, place the high shelf on the scratching post near a cupboard or other high furniture to give your cat additional "treetop" territory.
• British shorthair cats do not need the addition of upholstered and lined caves on scratching posts. Because of their dense fur, these felines do not typically seek warm, cozy nests as much as some other breeds.
• Some cats prefer to sharpen their claws on real tree bark. If you can use trunk pieces from a real tree, your cat will be pleased. Look for tree sections that have a strong trunk with sturdy branches that subdivide enough to create sitting areas.
• If you have several cats, offer them as many scratching and climbing posts as you can afford or accommodate in your home.

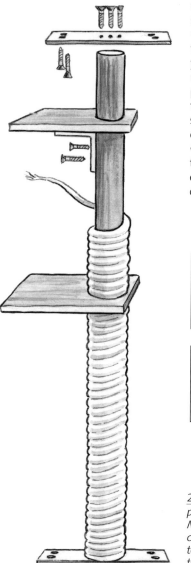

3| *This is the best way to secure the rope to the post.*

4| *The holes for the seats should be 8 inches (2 cm) from the edge of the narrow end.*

2| *Scratching post: A scratching post is a must for all indoor cats. More than just a place to sharpen claws, it is a tree to climb on, a toy to chase around, and a place to sleep and dream.*

Healthy Nutrition for British Shorthairs

To maintain excellent health, cats, like humans, need complete and balanced nutrition; however, the nutrient requirements of cats are vastly different from our own, which is why they cannot remain healthy solely on table scraps and people food. Having evolved as carnivores, cats must eat meat. They also require more protein than either humans or dogs, and a certain amount of a particular amino acid called taurine in their daily diet. Most mammals can synthesize sufficient amounts of this essential amino acid in their own bodies, but cats cannot. A taurine deficiency can lead to eye and heart diseases. Commercial cat foods typically contain added amounts of taurine, but dog foods contain an insufficient amount to keep cats healthy. This is one reason why you should never feed a cat dog food exclusively.

British shorthairs love to watch what is going on from a safe distance.

Nutritional Facts

If you are inclined to spoil your cat with home-cooked meals, it is important to know about the various nutritional components cats need before whipping up your own recipes. Any imbalance, whether too much or too little, can cause nutritional disorders. Most commercial cat foods today are well researched, test-fed to live animals, and guaranteed to provide "complete and balanced" nutrition for specific feline life stages. They take the guesswork out of how much and what to feed your cat. It is important to know that cooking a nutritionally complete and balanced meal from scratch for a cat requires the knowledge of an expert, plus a lot of time and effort. Portions of home-cooked meals are fine as an occasional supplement, so long as you watch your kitty's waistline, but arbitrarily feeding home-cooked meals routinely or exclusively is an unsafe practice because of the risk of nutritional deficiencies or excesses. An exception to this would be the case of a cat that is allergic to ingredients in commercial foods and home-cooked meals might be recommended as part of the treatment, but only under the direct supervision of a veterinarian or animal nutrition expert.

Following are just a few facts to keep in mind when offering your cat's daily diet:

Meat

Feral cats get their vitamins and minerals by eating small prey animals, such as mice and other rodents. They derive important minerals, such as calcium, and other nutrients from the bones of their prey and from the vegetable material contained in the stomachs of their prey. Feeding a house cat a pure meat diet can lead to nutritional deficiencies because the other components are lacking. The lack of calcium, for example, can cause mobility problems and bone fractures. Too much phosphorus, on the other hand, can inhibit calcium metabolism and absorption. In commercial cat foods, calcium

Nothing can distract a feline youngster from enjoying a meal of cream of wheat.

and many other essential components typically come from meats, ground bone meal, and other animal by-products. Vitamins and minerals that aren't supplied in the natural ingredients are routinely added to the mix during or after processing to ensure adequate amounts for a cat's daily needs. If you insist on offering people foods on occasion, remember to *never* feed your cat raw meats of any variety. Raw or under-cooked meats carry the potential risk of disease from bacteria and parasites, including the ones that cause salmonella infection and toxoplasmosis.

Fish

If you choose to offer fish on occasion, cook it and remove the bones. Feeding cats raw fish exclusive of other foods can cause a thiamine (vitamin B_1) deficiency. This is because an enzyme, called *thiaminase,* found in many kinds of raw fish, can destroy thiamine in the body and produce degenerative disease in the cat's central nervous system.

Signs of thiamine deficiency include appetite loss, vomiting, seizures, and loss of coordination.

Too much red tuna can also pose problems, leading to vitamin E deficiency. Some tuna is acceptable; a lot is not. Avoid offering tuna for humans and cat foods rich in red tuna meat exclusive of other flavors and varieties. An all-fish diet of this sort can lead to a condition called "yellow fat disease," which involves a buildup of yellow, lumpy fat deposits under the skin. Although commercial fish- and tuna-based cat foods contain adequate thiamine, vitamin E, and other supplements to guarantee complete and balanced nutrition, rotating these flavors with others varieties containing beef, chicken, turkey, lamb, etc., is recommended.

Organ Meats
As a rule, I advise against feeding organ meats because the organs store and metabolize all kinds of unhealthy food components. Beef hearts are the only exception to this rule. Feeding a cat too much liver can lead to a toxic accumulation of too much vitamin A, which may cause joint problems and bone deformations.

Cereals
Cereals such as rice, oats, and other grains make up a good portion of commercial cat foods. They supply needed energy in the form of carbohydrates and bulk in the form of fiber.

Eggs
While eggs are a good source of protein and fat for cats, they should be cooked first and never fed raw. In fact, some breeders recommend adding a well-cooked whole egg to the diet once or twice a week to make the coat shiny.

Raw eggs carry the risk of salmonella infection; raw egg whites contain a protein, called *avidin*, that can interfere with the body's absorption of the vitamin biotin, a member of the B complex family.

Milk and Water
Milk is a food and must not be considered a substitute for water. Like many people, many adult cats lose the ability to metabolize the lactose in milk and may develop diarrhea when they drink it.

Cats need fresh water daily. Make sure the water bowl is stable and heavy enough not to be spilled. On a hot day, a few ice cubes in the water provides a cool treat.

Forbidden Foods
Following is a list if foods that should be avoided:
• Raw or undercooked meats and fish (risk of infection with bacteria and parasites)
• Pickled herring (too much salt can cause intestinal upset)
• Bones (can splinter into sharp pieces and get lodged in the throat or intestinal tract)
• Spicy food leftovers (can cause severe digestive upset)
• Spiced cheese (can lead to digestive upset)
• Sweets (too much sugar can cause diarrhea)
• Chocolate (can be toxic in large quantities)
• Alcohol (is toxic in even small quantities)
• Dog food (doesn't contain enough protein or taurine to maintain feline health)
• Garbage scraps (if it's not fit for you to eat, it's not fit for your cat)

Commercial Cat Foods

There are still many people who insist on home-cooked meals for their cats. I do not share this opinion. No individual is truly able to produce a precisely balanced diet that serves the feline nutritional requirements completely. The process of cooking alone destroys a large part of the vitamins, minerals, and trace elements and the dosages of all ingredients turn out to be largely incorrect.

Commercial cat foods, on the other hand, offer a fully balanced meal, exactly prescribed for our feline friends. Of course, it's okay to create variety and serve your pet both by supplementing a mainstay commercial diet with an occasional home-cooked meal. Just make sure your cat doesn't consume more calories than it expends in a normal day's activity; otherwise, you'll wind up with a fat cat with all of the health risks, such as diabetes, heart disease, and joint problems, that go along with obesity.

Commercial cat foods come in three basic types: canned, dry (or kibbled), and semimoist. The type you choose to feed is largely a matter of convenience. When selecting a food, choose one that is guaranteed on the label to offer complete and balanced nutrition for your cat's particular life stage, whether it's a kitten, adult, or a pregnant or lactating queen. Because a cat's nutritional needs can change with each life stage, its diet must be adjusted accordingly.

Canned foods: These come in myriad flavors. Choose the brand that lists the highest amount of meat over fillers. When feeding canned foods, remove leftovers from cans and store them in plastic or other storage containers in the refrigerator. Do not keep the leftovers longer than one or two days. Most cats will refuse to eat chilled food straight from the refrigerator, always warm leftovers to room temperature by heating in the microwave oven or by placing the storage container in hot water.

Dry cat foods: These are manufactured by removing approximately 85 percent of the moisture content in the ingredients. This process makes kibbled diets a much more concentrated food, and your cat must consume more water to help the digestive system function smoothly. Fresh water access is an essential addition to dry food meals. Dry foods have a long shelf life, but once opened and exposed to air, light, and humidity, their nutritional value can deteriorate rapidly. To avoid this, store these foods in a cool, dry place, preferably in a recloseable container.

Cats enjoy nibbling on grass, perhaps because it acts as a natural purgative, helping to clear the digestive system of excess hair.

Semimoist foods: These nugget-shaped foods contain more moisture than dry foods, but not as much as canned foods. They are designed to combine the convenience of dry foods with the palatability of wet foods;

With a slightly grumpy expression, this cat waits for the disturbance to pass so she can

however, their convenient, single-meal, foil packaging makes them more expensive.

How Much Food Is Enough?

The amount of food any British short-hair cat will need varies with each individual and depends largely on age, health, temperament, and activity level. A highly active, playful British shorthair will burn a lot more calories than a slow, placid one. If your cat puts on a layer of fat, you may need to reduce the size of its meals. However, it's perfectly permissible and desirable for British shorthairs to carry a moderate amount of fat cushioning on their body, because this is part of the overall look of the breed. If you gently palpate the cat's sides, you should be able to feel, but not see, the ribs. If you can see the outline of the ribs, the cat is too thin and needs an increase in food intake.

Kittens

During their growth phases, young cats need a lot more calories than adults. For the first six months, feed kittens several small meals each day. For their first full year, feed a feline growth formula designed to deliver the extra protein and nutrients kittens need for optimal growth and development. To aid in the transition from mother's milk to solid foods, temporarily offer the kitten some meat-based baby food. Moisten kibbled kitten food with a warm, diluted mixture of evaporated milk and water. Beginning at seven months of age, divide the rations into two meals a day, just as you would for adult cats.

continue her grooming in peace.

Nursing or Pregnant Queens

During the reproductive phases of a female cat's life, she needs a rich variety of foods and flavors to compensate for her higher energy demands. Choose an energy-dense commercial cat food especially formulated for pregnant and lactating queens. Remember, the quality of nutrition you provide for your queen will affect the kittens' entire lives. Toward the end of the pregnancy, divide the recommended daily ration into several small meals. During lactation, some breeders may recommend calcium supplements, but this generally is not necessary if you are feeding a high-quality reproduction formula food.

Aging British Shorthairs

As cats age, their ability to digest and use needed nutrients from their diet appears to decline. This means that healthy older cats, age eight and up, usually require foods designed to have greater digestibility and higher nutritional value. In some cases, returning a healthy senior cat to a "kitten chow" formula may even be appropriate; however, some older, less active cats, particularly ones inclined to put on pounds, may require a diet with less fat and less protein. Also, older cats experiencing declining kidney function will benefit from prescription diets available through veterinarians. These diets are lower in protein and are designed to put less stress on the kidneys. The choice of diet depends on your senior cat's individual health status, which can be best assessed by your veterinarian during the annual checkup.

Keeping Your British Shorthair Healthy

Infectious diseases can be easily prevented in this breed of cats by combining routine vaccinations with good nutrition and good hygiene. Frequent sanitation of litter boxes is an essential part of this regimen. Also, the sleeping quarters must be cleaned regularly and disinfected from time to time. If you add to this an annual checkup at the veterinarian's office, there is good reason to believe your cat will enjoy a long, healthy life.

Feline Illnesses and Disorders

Several potentially fatal infectious diseases common in cats are preventable today because of effective vaccines. For maximum effectiveness, most vaccines are designed to establish initial immunity

This is the best type of transport kennel because it provides cats with a sense of safety.

with one or more injections, followed by a booster shot once a year (see Vaccination Schedule, page 43). Should you suspect an illness, or observe any unexplained changes in your cat's behavior, take your cat to a veterinarian right away for examination. The most common feline illnesses and disorders include:

Feline distemper: Also called feline panleukopenia virus (FPV) and feline infectious enteritis (FIE), this highly contagious, destructive disease is not related to canine distemper. Without early treatment, the disease is usually fatal. Symptoms include vomiting, diarrhea, listlessness, fever, lack of appetite, dehydration, and a tender abdomen. Often, an infected cat will crouch in a stiff, hunched-over manner.

Feline upper respiratory diseases: Feline viral rhinotracheitis (FVR), which is caused by a herpes virus, and feline calicivirus (FCV) both produce similar symptoms of eye and nasal discharge, appetite loss, listlessness, and sneezing. FCV often causes inflammation of the mouth and throat, which makes eating even more difficult for the sick cat. Mortality rates are highest among kittens and older cats, and survivors can become carriers. Both infections are easily prevented by regular vaccination.

Viral Diseases

Feline Leukemia Virus (FeLV): FeLV is caused by a retrovirus that attacks the immune system, leaving the cat susceptible to recurring infections and various cancers, such as leukemia. Symptoms vary but may include listlessness, poor

Ideal Vaccination Schedule*

Disease	1st Vaccination	2nd Vaccination	3rd Vaccination	Booster
Panleukopenia	6–8 weeks	10–12 weeks	16 weeks	yearly
Calicivirus	6–8 weeks	10–12 weeks	16 weeks	yearly
Rhinotracheitis	6–8 weeks	10–12 weeks	16 weeks	yearly
Chlamydiosis	6–8 weeks	10–12 weeks	16 weeks	yearly
Rabies	12–16 weeks	64–68 weeks		triannually
Leukemia	10–12 weeks	16 weeks		yearly

* NOTE: The age of the cat, type of vaccine, and route of administration influence the number of vaccinations required. Follow your veterinarian's recommendations.

appetite, weight loss, and enlarged lymph nodes. Infected cats may appear healthy for years before showing signs of illness. A test is available to determine whether cats are positive or negative for the virus. All breeding animals should be tested and certified free of the disease. Once contracted, the disease is incurable, but an effective vaccine exists.

Feline Infectious Peritonitus (FIP): The cause of this fatal infection is a coronavirus. Scientists are still debating the reliability of early diagnosis since the presence of antibodies in the blood is inconsistent. The manner of transmission is also varied and complicated. Although a nasal vaccine is available, most veterinarians recommend it only if the exposure threat is high, as in a cattery or a multicat household.

Feline Immunodeficiency Virus (FIV): Also called feline AIDS, this infectious disease is species-specific, meaning that it *cannot* be transmitted from cats to humans. The disease weakens the immune response of cats enough so that secondary complications may set in and cause serious illness and death. Symptoms may include general lethargy, weight loss, and chronic infections, especially of the gums. Bite wounds appear to be the main mode of transmission among cats. Blood tests can determine FIV status, but no cure and no approved vaccine are available. The best prevention is to keep your British shorthair indoors. Also, all cats should be tested for FIV (and FeLV) before being brought into a household with other cats.

Rabies: This fatal virus can be transmitted from cats to humans through bite wounds or through contact with infected saliva. Because of the threat to human lives, rabies vaccination is required by law in most localities. Symptoms may include fearful behavior, personality changes, aggression, paralysis, and excessive salivation.

Feline Chlamydiosis: Also called feline pneumonitis, this highly contagious disease results in swelling and inflammation of the eye area and prolapse of the third eyelid, called the *nictitating membrane.* A vaccine is available.

Other Disorders

Feline Lower Urinary Tract Disease (FLUTD): Also called feline urologic syndrome or FUS, this condition involves the formation of tiny mineral crystals in the cat's urethra, the tube that eliminates urine from the bladder. If the crystals are large enough, they may block the urethra completely, preventing urination and posing a potentially life threatening situation. Symptoms of FLUTD may include urinating in unusual places, straining to urinate, passing bloody urine, visiting the litter box frequently, and licking the genital area excessively. Most cats recover with prompt treatment, but recurrences are common.

Ringworm: Not a worm at all, this disorder is really a fungal infection of the skin. Symptoms include hair loss in distinct spots, followed by scaling and pustules at the head, neck, and leg. Because the fungus is contagious to humans, infected cats require prompt veterinary treatment. A vaccine is available.

Toxoplasmosis: This protozoan disease is of concern to pregnant women, because the transmitted organism can cause birth defects. Fortunately, most humans have been exposed to this organism sometime in their lives and have developed antibodies to protect them against the disease. As a precaution, pregnant women should take a blood test to confirm their antibody titer. If the pregnant woman shows no previous exposure, she should also have her cat tested. Because infections can occur through contact with feces eliminated by an infected cat, pregnant women, as a precaution, should wear gloves when cleaning the litter box.

Internal Parasites

The most common internal parasites found in cats are roundworms, hookworms, and tapeworms. Heartworms, common in dogs, rarely infest cats, except in some humid areas, where mosquitoes are a major problem. Because certain kinds of worms can be passed from the mother to the kittens, the general recommendation is to have all kittens checked for internal parasites during their first visit to the veterinarian.

Tapeworms, the most common internal parasite to plague cats, are transmitted primarily by fleas. Sometimes, you can easily spot signs of tapeworm infestation by examining the feces or the anal hair, where you may see tapeworm segments, which look like tiny grains of white rice. Treatment includes proper deworming medication, followed by effective flea control to prevent reinfestation.

External Parasites

Fleas, lice, mites, and ticks are all guilty of transmitting diseases or causing severe itching and scratching. Immaculate hygiene in the feline quarters, including frequent cleaning of pet bedding, is the best prevention. Symptoms may include scratching and head shaking. Fleas leave behind their excrement, which looks like fine grains of black sand, in the cat's fur. Some cats are allergic to flea bites and will scratch excessively to the point of causing patchy hair loss and crusty sores.

If you suspect your cat carries any parasites, consult your veterinarian for proper treatment. Effective flea control measures involve selecting products that are designed to kill adult fleas *and* prevent the eggs and larvae from

Seniors enjoy the loving devotion of a feline friend to fill their need for companionship and combat loneliness.

maturing into more fleas. The arsenal includes dips, shampoos, sprays, powders, and flea collars, which can be used to kill fleas on the animal, and room foggers, yard treatments, and carpet treatments, which are designed to kill and control fleas in the cat's environment. In addition, some highly effective but expensive once-a-month flea control medications are now available by prescription through your veterinarian. One is Program®, which is given orally by mixing it in the cat's food.

Another is Advantage®, a topical drug applied to the back of the cat's neck. With Program®, fleas bite the cat, ingest the drug, and lay infertile eggs, thus halting flea reproduction. Because Advantage® kills adult fleas that jump on the cat for up to one month, it is a better choice for cats that are allergic to flea bites.

Certain shampoos and flea products designed for use on dogs are too strong for cats and may cause severe, even fatal, reactions.

HOW-TO: Administering First Aid

When your cat is ill or injured, you may need to administer first aid before transporting it to the veterinary hospital. If your cat strongly resists your attempts to help, restrain it safely by wrapping it in a towel, leaving only the head sticking out.

Taking the Temperature
Drawing 1

This task is best performed by a veterinarian, but at times, you may need to do it yourself. Enlist the help of another person, if possible, so that one person can restrain the cat and lift the tail, while the other person carefully inserts the thermometer. First, coat the thermometer with a little Vaseline, then insert it into the anus about an inch (25 mm), using a gentle twisting motion and keeping the thermometer horizontal. Use a rectal, digital thermometer designed for cats or human infants. A cat's normal body temperature is 100 to 102. 5°F (37.8–39°C). If the temperature reads below or above this range, consult a veterinarian.

Administering Pills
Drawing 2

Hold the cat's head in your hand and press lightly on the corners of the mouth to gently force open the jaws. With the other hand, place the pill as far back on the tongue as possible in one quick motion. Quickly close the cat's mouth and stroke the throat to induce it to swallow the medicine.

Administering Liquid Medications

Pull up the medicine in an eyedropper or a syringe without the needle. Hold the cat's head in the same manner as for pilling, but squeeze the liquid slowly through the side of the mouth, allowing the animal enough time to swallow. Take care not to squeeze liquid into the mouth

too forcefully or too quickly; doing so may cause the cat to aspirate some of the medicine into the lungs, which can lead to pneumonia.

Administering Eye Medication
Drawing 3

Hold the cat's head firmly and gently pull the lower lid down carefully with your finger. With the other hand, drop the medication into the middle of the lowered lid. Close the eye gently and massage the lid lightly to spread the medication.

Administering Ear Drops
Drawing 4

Pull the ear flap gently backwards and allow the drops of medication to trickle into the ear. Avoid touching the ear with the medicine bottle tip, because the applicator must stay clean. After administering the drops, massage the ear lightly between thumb and forefinger to distribute the medication, *before* the cat has an opportunity to shake its head

1 Taking a cat's temperature is more easily accomplished by two people; one person holds the cat, while the other gently inserts the thermometer.

and fling out the ear drops. Never poke anything, such as a cotton swab, into the delicate ear canal.

Insect Bites and Bee Stings

If you can locate the stinger of a wasp or bee in your cat's paw, try to remove it with tweezers. If the sting causes swelling, make a compress by placing ice cubes, wrapped in cloth, to the area. If your cat gets stung inside the

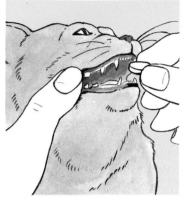

2] *Place the pill as far back on the tongue as possible.*

mouth, consult a veterinarian immediately—swelling inside the mouth and throat can obstruct the airway.

Cuts and Bite Wounds

Clean small, minor wounds carefully with clean water and a cloth to remove dirt, then consult a veterinarian. For major wounds, control severe bleeding by applying gentle pressure directly to the wound site, using your hand and a clean cloth. If you have a sterile compress, place it on the wound and secure it firmly with bandage strips or adhesive tape. Significant blood loss can lead to shock and death. Transport the animal to a veterinarian immediately.

Transporting an Injured Cat

Wrap a blanket carefully around the injured cat, lift it with the blanket, and lay it flat inside a transport container or box. Place the cat on the uninjured side. *Never* pick up an injured cat

by placing your hands under the belly; this will only worsen any injuries to the thorax or abdominal areas. During transport, keep the cat warm.

Poisoning

If a cat has ingested a poisonous substance, it may appear apathetic, it may stagger, or it may drool. It may also exhibit partial paralysis. Bloody urine or diarrhea may be signs of progressed poisoning. Get to an animal hospital as quickly as possible. Do not induce vomiting unless an expert advises you to do so, as some substances can cause more harm coming back up. If you know what agent caused the poisoning, call the hospital as you prepare to transport the cat, if possible. The veterinarian can give you proper first aid instructions. This will also give the clinic personnel time to prepare the right antidote for your emergency arrival.

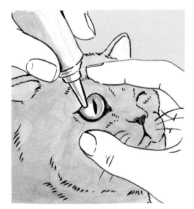

3] *Pull the lower lid down and place the drop in the middle of the lid.*

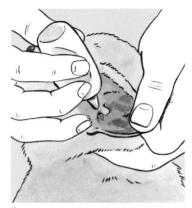

4] *Allow the drops to trickle into the ear, then follow with a gentle massage.*

Heat Stroke

As a rule, cats seek shade during hot weather. If they cannot escape the heat, they may suffer heat stroke. A cat suffering from heat stroke begins to breathe rapidly with an open mouth and becomes lethargic and weak. As a first aid measure, wrap the cat in wet towels or sponge it off with tepid water. Transport for emergency medical treatment. As a preventive measure, *never* leave your cat inside a car that is parked in the sun, not even with the windows cracked.

Drowning

The danger of drowning exists mainly where the water's edge is steep, making it difficult or impossible for a cat to climb out. Although cats can swim, they will succumb to exhaustion after a time if they fail to find a way out of the pool or pond. For this reason, swimming pools are quite dangerous, and pets should be supervised around pools.

47

Ear mites: These mites may try to make a home in your cat's ears and in the process cause severe inflammation. Your veterinarian can diagnose these parasites quickly and prescribe the correct medications. Symptoms include frequent shaking of the head and scratching at the ears. Inside the ear flap, you may see a crumbly, waxy, brown discharge.

What You Need to Tell the Veterinarian

Whenever your cat shows any signs of illness or changes in behavior, write down your observations so you won't forget any details after you arrive at the veterinarian's. Here are some important questions you may be asked:
• Have you noticed a change in your cat's patterns of food and water intake?
• Have you observed any diarrhea or constipation?
• Have you observed your cat straining to urinate or making frequent trips to the litter box? Have you noticed any blood in the cat's urine?
• Has the cat vomited? How often?
• Does the cat scratch itself much?
• Does the cat cough or sneeze?

Preventing Hair Balls

Self-grooming leads to an accumulation of hair in the cat's stomach, which sometimes is regurgitated as a hair ball. Occasional hair balls are normal and usually pose no problem, unless the cat vomits them too frequently, or unless a blockage develops in the cat's intestinal tract. To prevent complications, it is a good idea to administer an over-the-counter hair ball remedy from time to time. These preparations, available at pet supply stores, help lubricate the digestive tract so that hair moves through more easily and gets eliminated with the feces.

From kittens to cats, all enjoy climbing trees as a favorite pastime.

Sexual Maturity

Although British shorthairs are not among the early maturing felines, most males and females will be sexually mature by the time they are 15 months old.

Females: The first heat cycle has begun when your cat acts even sweeter than ever, when she rolls on the floor, intoning her "calls," and just about turns somersaults. This behavior increases for about a week and then diminishes slowly.

Toms: The male announces his sexual maturity by caterwauling to the local females and exhibiting a desire to roam in search of mates. Also, his urine odor intensifies. Soon, spraying (page 30) will follow. Depending on his personality and territory, he may spray his favorite objects. This odor is extremely unpleasant to humans and difficult to remove. Castration can help reduce or eliminate this undesirable male tendency before the behavior becomes firmly established.

Neutering and Spaying

Castrating or neutering the male involves removing the testicles. Spaying the female involves removing the ovaries, tubes, and uterus. The surgical procedure in the female cat is more complicated and expensive, because the abdomen is opened; however, the one-time cost of the surgery is still far cheaper than the cumulative expenses for raising successive litters of kittens. Both procedures render cats unable to reproduce and help eliminate undesirable sexual behavior, making them more suitable as house companions. For example, a spayed female will no longer exhibit annoying behavior associated with being "in heat," and the neutered male is less likely to spray and act aggressively. While most veterinarians still advise waiting until a cat is at

Only a small insect of some sort could interrupt the climbing antics of this lovely blue British shorthair youngster.

least six months old before spaying or neutering, recent studies have shown that altering cats at an earlier age is safe and does not adversely affect maturity, as was once thought.

Besides altering sexual behavior, the benefits of spaying and neutering are many. For the female, spaying decreases the chance that she may develop breast cancer later in life. For the male, castration decreases the chance of developing prostate cancer. Without the natural desire to roam in search of a mate, and perhaps be exposed to disease, hit by a car, or injured in a fight, your cat is more likely to stay close to home and live a longer, healthier life.

Breeding British Shorthairs

If you are interested in breeding your British shorthairs, memorize the breed standard and contact an experienced breeder near you. The association in which your cat is registered can provide information about breeders, breed standards, and breed clubs in your area.

Most people understand that much misery exists in the lives of felines throughout the world, simply because there are not enough good homes to go around for all cats. For this reason alone, it is irresponsible for people to breed cats solely because "kittens are so cute" or because they want their children to witness "the miracle of birth." It is equally unjustified to breed cats with the expectation of making a great deal of money, because there is no tangible profit in breeding if you are a conscientious breeder. It is a costly, and sometimes heart-breaking, hobby. Here are a few reasons that *are* considered valid justification for breeding:
• You want to improve and enhance the British shorthair breed.
• You want to own and show breed standard cats.
• You have lots of spare time (Kittens require much time and attention daily).
• You have lots of space, preferably a spare room just for the growth phase of the kittens.
• Costs, such as stud fees, veterinary fees, food, etc., are no obstacle for you.

Breed Standards

Before you begin, carefully study the breed standard set forth by the breed association(s) in which your cat is registered. A breed standard is sort of a written blueprint of ideals judges use when comparing cats of the same breed in competition. The cat that best conforms to these ideals wins in a cat show.

Also, when you're just starting out, seek advice from other cat fanciers and breeders who've been in the business for a long time. Most people who breed quality cats also show them at cat shows. Participating in show competition is essential for establishing and promoting the reputation of a breeder's cattery, or registered breeding stock. Another good way to learn and to meet breeders is to visit as many cat shows as possible and talk with the exhibitors. Some experienced breeders will allow enthusiastic novices to co-own breeding stock with them, while learning and serving a sort of informal breeder's apprenticeship.

Breeding Strategies

Breeders often try to concentrate good qualities in a bloodline by breeding related cats to each other. Unfortunately, this practice can also concentrate any bad genes along with the desirable ones. The practice is called "inbreeding" if the cats are closely related, such as mother to son or father to daughter. It is typically referred to as "linebreeding" when more distant relatives are mated. At one point during the British shorthair's early history, the pool of purebred stock had dwindled to such small numbers that breeders found it necessary to "cross-breed" their cats, or mate them with cats of different breeds, to increase the gene pool, and thus avoid the unhealthy effects of too much inbreeding. This may also be done, when permitted by the cat fancy's governing bodies, to create new colors and varieties. Currently, the largest association, CFA, allows no outcrosses for the British shorthair.

Stud Fees

Stud fees may range from $300 to $500 or more, depending on the male's number of wins in the show ring and on his proven status as a stud. Fees also vary from one geographic region to another.

If the mating did not result in a pregnancy, inform the owner of the stud male at least by the seventh week. In such a case, the owner of the queen can expect a repeated mating attempt at no extra charge. Repeated matings are quite common because transporting the queen to the tom, particularly if the distance is long, often causes the queen to go out of heat. In some cases, the stud owner may need to house the queen for a considerable period of time to ensure a successful mating.

Choosing the Right Mate

Several months prior to any planned mating, both owners need to clearly communicate all terms of their agreement. When choosing a mate, spare no expense, and do not make distance a factor of choice. A breeding mate should not be selected simply because he "lives just around the corner." Of course, both animals should be registered British shorthairs. Ask to see the pedigree of any prospective mate. The more names that are prefixed by Ch. or Gr. Ch., for champion and grand champion, the better the chances that one or more of the progeny may turn out to be winners, too.

Breeding choices should be carefully planned and based on the *phenotypes* of both animals, or their external characteristics, as well as on the *genotypes*, or the internal or pedigree- and genetic-related characteristics. At least one of the partners should have previous mating experience. Both prospective parents should be tested and certified free of feline leukemia virus and feline AIDS. They should also be up to date on all vaccinations and be free of internal and external parasites.

Introduction and Approach

Because the queen is usually taken to the tom, preferably on the second day of her heat, the stud male owner assumes all responsibility for the care, food, and housing of the queen during her stay. An experienced breeder will know not to place a queen in front of a previously unfamiliar stud without giving the two a chance to get acquainted. A sudden, face-to-face meeting could place the female at the mercy of the stronger male. A grate or other type of divider should separate the two animals in the area where the mating will take place. This division allows them to view and sniff each other. Ideally, the quarters should offer the queen a place to retreat for security. When the time seems right, and the two animals have had sufficient contact to accept each other, the divider is removed to allow mating to take place.

This softly cushioned nest box is cozy and comfortable for your queen.

"Sleep or play?" that is the question.

The stud owner should remain present and supervise the proceedings so that neither cat gets hurt.

Mating

If the queen reacts calmly and purrs in response to the stud's advances, mating may occur within a few hours or on the following day. Unlike most mammals, cats are "induced ovulators," which means that the sex act must occur before eggs are released from the ovaries. The tom's penis is lined with tiny barbs that stimulate the inside of the queen's vagina, aiding in the eggs' release. Immediately after copulation, the queen typically yowls a high-pitched "sound of indignation," rolls over quickly, and tries to swipe her paw at the stud's face. This behavior is thought to be due to the intense stimulation needed to induce ovulation.

If all goes according to nature's plan, the mating rituals and enactments usually take about two or three days.

Pregnancy

During the first couple of weeks after mating, you can only guess whether your cat is pregnant. At first, she might sleep a lot and behave more calmly than before the mating. At around three weeks of gestation, the first visible sign of pregnancy appears, a change in the coloration of the nipples; they turn pink and appear somewhat enlarged. A veterinarian can confirm the pregnancy by palpating the queen's abdomen, but unless you are trained, you should avoid doing this yourself because of the risk of potential injury to the babies inside.

By the fourth or fifth weeks, the queen's sides begin to fill in, depending on the number of fetuses in the litter.

No problem for kittens—they can do both at once.

An average litter numbers three to six offspring. The gestation time for a cat ranges from 63 to 66 days, up to 70 days is considered normal.

Figure out the due date, and check with your veterinarian to make sure he or she will be available at the anticipated time of birth. Also, to help ensure that your queen gets the nutrition she needs, and her kittens get their best start, remember to feed her a high-quality feline reproduction and growth formula during her entire pregnancy and lactation.

The Nesting Box

Two weeks before the expected birth, offer your cat Mom a nesting box (drawing page 51). Following are directions to prepare one:

• Use a strong cardboard box approximately 14 inches wide by 10 inches high (35.5 × 25 cm).

• On one side of the carton, cut out a section to make an entry for Mom. Leave an edge of about 4 inches (10.2 cm) so the newborns won't fall out.

• Place a thick layer of newspapers on the bottom of the box, then put some towels or cloth on top. This bedding will be washed and changed or discarded after the birth.

• Place the nesting box in a quiet, draft-free, and rather dark area of the house, away from foot traffic and other pets.

• Place food and water bowls and a litter box nearby for the queen.

The Birth

If you observe closely, you will see that cats usually announce an impending birth. The expectant mother may act nervous and restless; or she may not let you out of her sight. She may run back and forth between the litter box and her nesting box, or she may slip into open closets or drawers so she can build her own nesting site. If you observe her pawing or scratching in this manner (the nesting instinct), the big event is near.

Preparations for the Delivery

Have the following items assembled and ready for the birth:
• a pair of scissors, which should be disinfected with alcohol
• a scale for weighing the newborns
• paper and pencil for notations regarding the delivery
• sterile pieces of cloth or towels
• an eyedropper or small ear syringe for clearing airways

Mom lies patiently as her kittens climb all over her.

• an antiseptic solution for cleansing instruments and umbilical cord stumps
• a heating pad for warming the nesting box

Stages of Labor

Mucus secretion and fluid from a broken amniotic sac will be the first signs of a birth in progress. If this is the first litter, the queen might vocalize once or twice with the birth of the first kittens. Just before the start of the birthing, you may notice a change in the shape of the abdomen. This happens because the entire packet of kittens shows up as an outline along the flanks of the cat. Also, the queen's hair coat may stand up, and her breathing may quicken with increasing labor.

Birthing

While many cats seem to want to have their owners close by during the birth to offer calming encouragement and praise, some do not. If your cat is one that does not, keep a respectful distance, but watch the proceedings, in case it becomes necessary for you to step in and help. Never leave a cat alone during this time.

The first kitten should be born three to four hours after the onset of labor. In most cases, the entire litter has arrived after about six hours. If there is more delay, call your veterinarian, especially if the queen seems weak, restless, lethargic, or distressed.

Kittens are born head or tail first, usually still surrounded by the amniotic sac, which the queen tears open upon birth. Then she licks her baby clean and, in doing so, she stimulates its breathing. Instinctively, she clears the newborn's nose and mouth passages with her rough tongue. She also usually will bite through the umbilical cord, severing it herself. After each kitten is born, another labor contraction expels the afterbirth, which the queen usually eats. Do not be alarmed by this, as this is her natural way of cleaning the nest of birth odors that might attract predators. There will be one placenta for each kitten born. Count them and make sure all are expelled, as a retained placenta can cause a serious infection.

How to Assist During the Birth

As a rule, cats do not need help when they give birth. However, if the mother does not appear to pay attention to the newborn you will need to step in and clear the kitten's airway. To do this, wipe away mucus and fluid from the nose and mouth of the tiny animal. Then, with freshly cleaned and disinfected hands, use your fingernails to sever the umbilical cord about an inch (25 mm) from the belly. This method is similar to the queen's bite. If you're squeamish about using your fingers, clamp or tie the cord about an inch (25 mm) from the kitten's navel, then use a pair of dull, disinfected scissors to cut the cord on the placental side.

If Mom still refuses to show any mothering instincts, you will need to rub the infant dry with warm towels. Then place the little one back against the mother's body so that she has a chance to get used to the newborn. After the kittens are born, change the bedding and clean the nesting box daily.

Growth and Development of the Kittens

British shorthair kittens look like fluff balls when they are first born. The thicker hairs of the undercoat stand out straight through the soft, silvery gray top coat. Those baby hairs disappear with time. Newborns weigh an average 3 to 5 ounces (100–150 g), and they grow quickly. During the first few days, the babies seem permanently attached to Mom's nipples, each one to its own reserved nipple.
• In only seven days, kittens can double their birth weight.
• At about eight to ten days, their eyes will open. All kittens of this breed have blue eyes at first, and only at about six weeks of age will the characteristically attractive copper colored eyes begin to appear.
• At two weeks of age, the kittens start crawling around and playing clumsily with their siblings.
• During the fourth week, the little ones leave the nest for the first time. Still stumbling and wobbly, they are out to discover the world.
• Depending on their mother's milk supply, you may need to supplement meals with kitten food beginning in the fourth or fifth week.
• Now it is also time for the mother to show them how to use the kitty litter box—Mom no longer wants to clean urine and fecal matter off their little rear ends.
• At six to eight weeks of age, kittens are ready to begin their vaccination schedule (see page 43).

Handling: At three weeks of age, begin gently handling and talking to the kittens a few minutes each day to help socialize them and get them accustomed to human contact. By doing so, you can expect to raise alert and trusting British shorthairs. Create a stress-free environment for the newborn litter—kittens will get nervous if they are exposed to constant interruption by humans and other house pets. Do not allow children to handle the kittens at this fragile stage, and even later on, unless you are present to supervise. A child's unintentional roughness can injure a delicate kitten.

Kittens develop normally and in an uncomplicated manner if they are raised in a secure and quiet environment. Perhaps you could place the mother and her kittens in a spare bedroom, or keep them safely confined in a child's playpen. Let your creativity run free—there are no set rules to getting it done right.

This cream-colored British shorthair can be expected to become a highly prized show cat.

Showing Your British Shorthair

Much discussion has revolved around the pros and cons of showing cats. One might think of it as a dream hobby come true, while another considers it borderline cruelty to animals because of the confinement and chaos the cat is subjected to. As a breeder and cat fancier, my personal opinion lies somewhere in the middle of the two extremes. I firmly believe that appropriate conditioning, care, and handling spares the animal most of the stress. If you're planning to show your cat, get it used to the show ring early in kitten classes. This will create a well-adjusted and adaptable adult, and it will help save you and your cat most of the stress.

Cat Show Organizations

In 1899 the first and oldest U.S. registry, the American Cat Association (ACA), was formed to keep records. Today, at least eight additional cat-registering associations exist in North America. (See list under Useful Addresses, page 62.)

What You Need to Know About Cat Shows

Judging Rings

In the U.S., judging takes place in *judging rings* set up in an area of the show hall where spectators can watch. A ring consists of a judging table with a row of cages behind it. When their class is called, exhibitors carry their cats to the ring and place them in a numbered cage.

In the ring, the judge removes each cat from its cage, places it on the table, and thoroughly examines it. The judge evaluates each cat according to how closely it matches the written standard of perfection for its particular breed, pattern, and color. After examining all cats in the ring in this manner, the judge hangs ribbons on the winners' cages, and the exhibitors come forward and carry their cats back to their benching stations.

Show Entry

While joining a cat club in your area that is affiliated with one of the cat-registering associations is not a requirement for showing, being a member gives you the opportunity to ask questions and learn from others with more experience. The association informs the membership well in advance of scheduled shows. Cat magazines also list show dates. To enter a show, you simply complete an entry form and return it to the appropriate address with the required entry fee.

Your first show is likely to be an "all-breed" show, where, as the name says, all cats, regardless of their breed, can compete. There are also specialty shows limited to just shorthaired or longhaired breeds. To earn points in any formal exhibition, your cat needs to be registered with the association sponsoring the show. Unaltered pedigreed cats begin in "open" classes and earn wins that count toward championships, grand championships, and other titles. Spayed and neutered cats compete separately for comparable championship titles, called "premiership" in the CFA. Many shows also have a household pet category for mixed breed or nonpedigreed cats, which must be spayed or neutered. Household pets are judged for their overall beauty, condition, and personality. Experimental breeds and colors of cats also get their chance to be seen, but only in nonchampionship status, generally classed as Provisional, Miscellaneous, New Breeds and Colors (NBC), or Any Other Variety (AOV).

Show Supplies and Preparation

The show committee provides a bench cage for your cat and a chair for you for the duration of the show. This is your *benching station*. The show flyer usually describes the cage dimensions. You'll want to bring some sheets or curtains to decorate the cage and provide your cat with a measure of privacy. You'll also need to bring cat food, food and water bowls, a kitty toilet, bedding, cage decorations, grooming supplies, a grooming table (a folding patio table works well), and a spray bottle of disinfectant for sterilizing the cage. Many shows provide kitty litter, but bring some along, just in case.

Although shows in the United States are not generally "vetted," it goes without saying that your cat must be free of fleas and disease before entering a show hall with other cats. In some cases, you may be asked to furnish proof of up-to-date vaccinations, so be prepared. A day or two before the show, you will want to give your cat a bath and trim its claws. If you usually powder the fur, as many exhibitors do to separate the hairs and add fluff and volume, be sure to thoroughly brush out all reside. Traces of powder left in the fur could be cause for disqualification.

Arriving at the Show

After you check in at the door and settle your cat in its assigned cage, read the show catalog schedule to determine when your cat will be judged. Keep your ears tuned to the public address system, and when you hear your cat's number called, carry your cat to the appropriate judging ring. Your number will be posted on top of one of the cages in the ring. Place your cat in the correct cage, then take a seat in the audience to quietly watch the judging.

Depending on how well your cat scored in the ring, it may be called back for finals. From among the top finalists are chosen the cats that will receive the highest awards: Best of Breed and Best in Show. Cats that win in the finals earn points based on the number of cats defeated at the show. These points count toward regional and national titles.

Point Scale for Show Cats

In the show ring, a British shorthair is judged on how closely it matches the breed standard adopted by the association governing the show. The standard assigns points for various features, with a total score of 100 possible, but rare. The chart on page 59 lists the Cat Fanciers' Association's point scores assigned for British shorthairs.

Benefits of Showing

Besides being fun and enjoyable, cat shows are an educational experience, whether you choose to be an exhibitor or simply a spectator. You can learn a lot about cat care simply by talking to other cat fanciers and by watching how they groom and handle their animals. Perhaps one of the best "perks" of cat shows is the time you get to spend shopping at the numerous vendors' displays selling cat-motif gifts, toys,

CFA Point Scores

Head (25)

Muzzle and Chin	5
Skull	5
Ears	5
Neck	5
Eye Shape	5

Body (35)

Torso	20
Legs and paws	10
Tail	5

Coat (20)

Texture, length, density	20

Color (20)

Eye color	5
Coat color	15

cat furniture, grooming aids, and accessories.

It's important to remember that the cat associations and related competitions exist primarily to promote responsible breeding and cat ownership. People who engage in the grueling business of breeding and showing cats do so because they love cats, not because they expect to make money. Indeed, most are lucky to break even after paying their travel expenses on the show circuit—veterinary bills, cat food, cat litter, stud fees, and so on. Finding the time to devote to transporting a show cat from city to city is also difficult for people who work full-time jobs. If, after visiting a few shows, you decide that this hobby is not for you after all, you still have a loyal and wonderful companion in your British shorthair to enjoy for years to come.

An experienced British shorthair tolerates a show without any signs of stress

Index

Dog and cat become best friends when they grow up together.

Useful Addresses and Literature

North American Cat Registries

American Association of
    Cat Enthusiasts (AACE)
P.O. Box 213
Pine Brook, NJ 07058
(201) 335-6717

American Cat Association
    (ACA)
8101 Katherine Avenue
Panorama City, CA 91402
(818) 781-5656

American Cat Fanciers
    Association (ACFA)
P.O. Box 203
Point Lookout, MO 65726
(417) 334-5430

Canadian Cat Association
    (CCA)
220 Advance Boulevard,
    Suite 101
Brampton, Ontario
Canada L6T 4J5
(905) 459-1481

Cat Fanciers' Association
    (CFA)
1805 Atlantic Avenue
P.O. Box 1005
Manasquan NJ 08736-
    0805
(908) 528-9797

Cat Fanciers' Federation
    (CFF)
Box 661
Gratis, OH 45330
(513) 787-9009

National Cat Fanciers'
    Association (NCFA)
20305 West Burt Road
Brant, MI 48614
(517) 585-3179

The International Cat
    Association (TICA)
P.O. Box 2684
Harlingen, TX 78551
(210) 428-8046

United Feline Organization
    (UFO)
P.O. Box 3234
Olympia, WA 98509-3234
(360) 438-6903

Other Associations

American Humane Society
P.O. Box 1266
Denver, CO 80201
(303) 695-0811

American Society for the
    Prevention of Cruelty to
    Animals (ASPCA)
424 East 92nd Street
New York, NY 10128
(212) 876-7700

Cornell Feline Health
    Center
Cornell University College
    of Veterinary Medicine
Ithaca, NY 14853
(607) 253-3414

The Delta Society
P.O. Box 1080
Renton, WA 98057
(206) 226-7357

The Humane Society of
    the United States
    (HSUS)
2100 L Street, NW
Washington, DC 20037
(202) 452-1100

Morris Animal Foundation
45 Inverness Drive, East
Englewood, CO 80112-
    5480
(800) 243-2345

Cat Magazines

CATS Magazine
Subscriptions:
P.O. Box 420240
Palm Coast, FL 32142-0240
(904) 445-2818
Editorial offices:
P.O. Box 290037
Port Orange, FL 32129-
    0037
(904) 788-2770

Cat Fancy
Subscriptions:
P.O. Box 52864
Boulder, CO 80322-2864
(303) 666-8504
Editorial offices:
P.O. Box 6050
Mission Viejo, CA 92690
(714) 855-8822

Cat Fancier's Almanac
Cat Fanciers' Association
1805 Atlantic Avenue
P.O. Box 1005
Manasquan, NJ 08736-
    0805
(908) 528-9797

Catnip (newsletter)
Tufts University School of
    Veterinary Medicine
Subscriptions:
P.O. Box 420014
Palm Coast, FL 32142-0014
(800) 829-0926
Editorial offices:
300 Atlantic Street,
    10th Floor
Stamford, CT 06901
(203) 353-6650

Books

Behrend, Katrin. *Indoor
    Cats.* Barron's
    Educational Series,
    Hauppauge, New York,
    1994

Behrend, Katrin and
    Wegler, Monika. *The
    Complete Book of
    Cat Care.* Barron's
    Educational Series,
    Hauppauge, New York,
    1991

Maggitti, Phil. *Guide to a
    Well-Behaved Cat.*
    Barron's Educational
    Series, Hauppauge,
    New York, 1993

Pinney, Chris. *Caring for
    Your Older Cat.*
    Barron's Educational
    Series, Hauppauge,
    New York, 1996

Rice, Dan, D.V.M. *The
    Complete Book of
    Cat Breeding.* Barron's
    Educational Series,
    Hauppauge, New York,
    1996

About the Photographer

The photos in this book were produced by Ulrike Schanz. She is a freelance photo design artist who specializes in animal portraiture.

About the Illustrator

Renate Holzner works as a freelance illustration artist in Regensburg. Her broad areas of expertise cover everything from line drawings to photo realistic illustrations and computer graphics.

About the Author

Friedhelm Lessmeier is a cat fancier who breeds British shorthairs under the registered cattery name of "Bavarians Blue " His many years of experience with British shorthair cat breeds has earned him uncounted national and international awards and recognition.

Acknowledgment

Author and publisher thank Dr. Franz-Josef Denninger and Dr. Rasso Selmaier for their expert review and advice of the chapters on nutrition and health.

Front Cover Photo

Big William from the author's cattery "Bavarians Blue," is an impressive, highly decorated winner of the title Grand International Champion, bred by the author.

Back Cover Photo

A lilac kitten, also bred by the author.

All inquiries should be addressed to:
Barron's Educational Series, Inc.
250 Wireless Boulevard
Hauppauge, NY 11788

International Standard Book No. 0-7641-0056-4

Library of Congress Catalog Card No. 96-54580

Library of Congress Cataloging-in-Publication Data
Lessmeier, Friedhelm.
   [*Kartäuser britisch Kurzhaar blau.* English]
   The British shorthair cat : everything about acquisitions, care, nutrition, behavior, health care, and breeding / Friedhelm Lessmeier ; color photographs by Ulrike Schanz ; illustrations by Renate Holzner ; consulting editor, Karen Leigh Davis.
      p.   cm. — (A complete pet owner's manual)
   Includes bibliographical references and index.
   ISBN 0-7641-0056-4
   1. British shorthair cat. I. Davis, Karen Leigh, 1953– . II. Title. III. Series.
SF449.BL4L4713   1997
636.8'22—dc21   96-54580
                                                CIP

Printed in Hong Kong

987654321

Important Advice

Scratches and bites are common injuries to those who handle cats frequently. A physician should be consulted when these injuries occur. It is absolutely essential that you complete all worming and vaccination schedules because the lack of immunization could lead to serious illness in cats and humans alike. Some diseases and parasites are transmitted from cats to humans. If your cat shows any symptoms of disease, consult a veterinarian. If in doubt about whether you can catch something from your cat, consult your personal physician and explain that you are a cat owner and describe the symptoms you have observed in your animal.

Some people are allergic to cat dander. If you have unexplained symptoms of sneezing or itching, but you are unsure whether you are allergic to cats, seek your physician's advice.

Cats can cause damage to other people's property, they can bite or scratch other people, and they can cause accidents. As a cat owner, consider your need for liability insurance as a matter of self-protection.

This friendship is not as unusual as it appears. It is fairly common for a naive British shorthair kitten to evoke protective maternal instincts in a dog, unless the dog was previously trained to chase cats.